Keepers
of the Sea

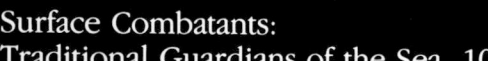

The United States Naval Institute, Annapolis, Maryland

Photographs © 1983 by Fred J. Maroon;
text © 1983 by Edward L. Beach

Library of Congress Cataloging in Publication Data

Maroon, Fred J.
  Keepers of the sea.

  1. United States. Navy.   I. Beach, Edward Latimer,
1918– . II. Title.
VA58.4.M37   1983   359'.00973   82-61291
(regular) ISBN 0-87021-727-5
(deluxe) ISBN 0-87021-736-4

Printed in the United States of America

First frontispiece:
A distant silhouette on a shimmering sea symbolizes the purpose of our navy. She has darkened ship for night steaming. Tomorrow she may be called on to go in harm's way. Her readiness for action is the proud heritage of many generations of navy men.

Second frontispiece:
Shortly after sunrise on a cloud-shrouded day in the Atlantic, today's ship of the line lies in the background haze. She is the USS Nimitz, *powered by two nuclear reactors, named in honor of the revered Pacific Fleet commander of World War II. Above her, in symbolic formation, is part of the awesome armament this single ship can fling into the skies. Sixteen planes are shown; she can carry more than ninety and launch them in minutes.*

Third frontispiece:
Navigation in an element to which this ship is unaccustomed: fog. The Whale, *an attack submarine, has just left New London, Connecticut, and is proceeding cautiously toward deep water. Like the* Nimitz, *she is nuclear powered, but her domain is beneath the surface instead of above. Taken together, the two ships represent the U.S. Navy's jump into three operational dimensions.*

Fourth frontispiece:
A special kind of aircraft carrier: the guided-missile frigate McInerney *is fitted for handling large helicopters carrying computer terminals, location devices, submarine-detecting sonobuoys and deep-diving homing torpedoes. Computers in both helo and frigate monitor the sonobuoys and can launch a torpedo automatically. The helo can land in bad weather by hooking on and being winched in.*

Fifth frontispiece:
A new flying boat, waterborne instead of airborne. The USS Pegasus *is driven by 26,000-hp gas turbines while on her foils and by two 670-hp diesels while hull borne. She has water-jet pumps instead of propellers and can make more than 50 knots on her foils. Her principal weapon is the Harpoon missile, mounted aft. She can use her foils in surprisingly heavy weather.*

Title page: *A U.S. cruiser, outward-bound into the sunset. Events half the world away may affect her. A radio message can send her anywhere. The navy was once known as our first line of defense, and it still is just that: a ship at sea is capable of graduated degrees of force that men on the ground or planes in the air cannot compass.*

Acknowledgments

This book began when Tom Ross and Rear Admiral David Cooney, in the Pentagon, approved the concept of a comprehensive view of today's U.S. Navy at sea. It became a reality through the confidence, courtesy and freedom extended to Ned Beach and me on all levels of the U.S. Navy.

To Admirals Tom Hayward and Jack Williams, as well as to Rear Admiral Bruce Newell and those under his command who were my day-to-day sponsors, I owe special thanks. Appreciation is also due Rear Admiral Hank Mustin for his enthusiastic cooperation, and to those many skippers and public affairs officers who gave so much while we were their working guests.

Lieutenant Eric Lofquist deserves particular thanks, as do the people who flew the helicopters and other aircraft that served as platforms for the aerial shots in this book. Captain Bruce Young was invaluable in explaining what my pictures really show. Tom Hall provided both support and physical assistance. Walter Heun, of E. Leitz, Inc., personally saw to it that I was never without perfect equipment. My agent, Louis Mercier, was, as always, the Rock of Gibraltar. The humor and willing energy of Richard Frasier, my photographic assistant, were vital. The U.S. Naval Institute staff gave us the benefit of their unique expertise in naval matters and were terrific in their support. And Chuck Hyman deserves a special tribute for the book's brilliant design.

Finally, my wife Suzy played a large part in making this book possible, not only by organizing the results of my expeditions but by providing strength at home during my absences.

Fred J. Maroon

I, too, owe many people for helping consummate the dream with which this book began. For their assistance with our coverage of naval air I am indebted to Wes McDonald, James Dennis and Dave Gist, and for my nitty-gritty experience on the flight deck I am particularly grateful to Bill Posnett and Don Miskill. The modern surface navy was extremely well represented by Carl Anderson and Ted Baker. In my own branch, Ron Thunman and Lee Watkins made me wish I could have one of the amazing submarine boats they are driving today. Mike Kubishen renewed my knowledge of replenishment-at-sea techniques, and Carl Trost laid out some of the worldwide problems he tackled in orchestrating the U.S. Navy's Indian Ocean effort. The assistance and enthusiasm of Lando Zech, Paul Malloy and Doug Sommer in the personnel and training area were infectious; and on the subject of projecting sea power on the land, Ed Simmons and George Worthington rendered the valuable service of their background and experience. Gordon Peterson, Ken Satterfield, George Vercessi, Tom Burgess, Juli Reynolds and Tony Hilton provided Fred and me with tremendous assistance in getting the pictures and contacts needed. At the U.S. Naval Institute, Tom Epley and Dick Hobbs were our mainstays; and Ron Amoss and Connie Buchanan, in their inimitable ways, tactfully and thoughtfully put it all together.

All of my family read what I wrote and gave valuable comments. They also merit a grateful mention on this very personal page.

Edward L. Beach

Dedication

To the everlasting memory of our classmates in high school and the Naval Academy who gave the full measure during World War II. May today's U.S. Navy, whose excellence stems largely from that war, ensure that their sacrifices will not have to be repeated.

Preface

From time immemorial, the purpose of a navy has been to influence, and sometimes to decide, issues on land. This was so with the Greeks of antiquity, the Romans, who created a navy to defeat Carthage, the Spanish, whose armada tried and failed to conquer England, and most eminently in the Atlantic and Pacific during two world wars. The sea has always given man inexpensive transport and ease of communication over long distances. It has also provided concealment, because being over the horizon meant being out of sight and effectively beyond reach. The sea has supplied mobility, capability and support throughout Western history, and those failing the sea power test—notably Alexander, Napoleon and Hitler—also failed the longevity one.

Traditionally, a navy sweeps in from a clear sea. Appearing quickly and unexpectedly, it becomes a presence that must be reckoned with. Sometimes a navy only demonstrates its potential, by lying in a sea lane or over the horizon, self-contained and benign. Sometimes it has to be less than friendly. Yet, in all conceivable situations, a navy must have the means to deal with whatever challenges it may face. Therefore, it must remain solidly in the forefront of modern technology.

During their war for independence, the rebelling American colonies early realized their need for strength on the sea, but the rather good little navy they built could not affect the outcome of the struggle. It took the much bigger navy of France to do that. Few Americans understand that the supremely important decision at Yorktown in 1781 required the timely arrival of a large French fleet, transferred from the Caribbean, and its subsequent victory over the English at the entrance to Chesapeake Bay. Yorktown stands in history as an almost perfect example of the use of sea power. It was also one of the few times England lost at sea. As of 1805 the world ocean was an English lake, and it remained so until 1914. The Royal Navy had accomplished its mission of protecting the nation, and Great Britain thereafter made full use of the sea hegemony she had gained. She fought piracy and the slave trade, kept the peace on the sea, and, of course, furthered her own colonial and commercial aspirations. It was said that the sun never set on the ensign of Great Britain.

Americans, those of us in North America at least, recognize England's navy as the father of ours. Our Continental navy took its customs and traditions from the Royal Navy, where many of its officers and men received their training. Our navy fought England's one more time, but otherwise went about its affairs during the nineteenth century in the shadow of the British protectorate (not, of course, during the War of 1812 and our Civil War). The bond of shared professionalism exists to this day.

Early morning sun in the Gulf of Mexico shines brightly on the USS Eisenhower *and two nuclear cruiser escorts. An entire battle group comprises dozens of ships scattered over many thousands of square miles. Seldom, nowadays, are any of its units this close together.*

18–19: *A little plaque on the teak deck planks reads, "Over this spot on 2 September 1945 the Instrument of Surrender of Japan to the Allied Powers was signed, thus bringing to a close the Second World War." The* Missouri *may return to service, for no non-nuclear missile can penetrate her armor.*

20–21: *The chief of naval operations (CNO) is a member of the Joint Chiefs of Staff and, by law, the president's principal adviser on naval matters. Since he must be able to reach any part of the navy on a moment's notice, communications requirements are enormous.*

Out of our Civil War came a significant American contribution to the science of modern navies: proofing the ironclad warship. The well-studied battle between Russian and Turkish fleets in 1853 at Sinope, on the northern coast of Asia Minor, had shown conclusively that wooden ships, no matter how sturdy, were no match for modern artillery firing explosive shells from rifled cannon. Iron sides had to be the answer. France is credited with the first ironclad warship, and England followed three years later. Both nations had extremely interested observers at Hampton Roads in March of 1862, when the Union's *Monitor* fought the Confederate *Virginia* (converted from the captured Union *Merrimack*).

The United States had, in fact, invented and proof-tested two new steam-powered warships, devoid of masts or sails and completely covered with iron sheathing. The *Monitor* was heavily armored, very low in freeboard, and mounted two powerful guns in a rotatable iron house, or turret. The high-sided *Virginia*, with ten somewhat smaller guns in an armored casemate, was the progenitor of the faster cruiser of later times. The two ironclads dueled for four hours, sometimes at point-blank range. The engagement ended in a standoff, yet, for all the cannonading, there were few injuries and no deaths on either side. The *Monitor*, conceived and designed by the expatriated Swede John Ericsson, was an entirely new concept in fighting ships. Thereafter, all ships of the type were known as monitors. They were widely imitated by all navies; as the most powerful and heavily armored ships that could be devised, they evolved into what became known as battleships. The development of the monitors followed in a tradition of innovation already established in the U.S. Navy. During the remaining years of the Civil War, a succession of monitors of the North and casemated ironclads of the South resulted from the search for able, seagoing fighting ships under the conditions created by the Industrial Revolution. The ironclads had opened a new era in naval warfare, and sails played no part in it. This changed the course of naval history. Rapid improvement in metallurgy and in steam engineering made the outcome inevitable.

The antenna array of the Belleau Wood. *Such arrays are the trademark of all warships.*

Facing: The business end of the world's largest communication system. With antennas like these the CNO (and thus the president) can communicate instantly with any naval commander anywhere.

In 1898 the United States had a first-class navy that acquitted itself with distinction against Spain, an ill-prepared and already declining naval power. During the next fifteen years, warships trebled in size, guns quadrupled in range, and speed and accuracy of fire ("hits per gun per minute") became a laborious fetish. The size and number of dreadnoughts, as battleships were then called (because of the success of the new British battleship of that name), became the measure of naval power.

Shortly after the turn of the century, England and Germany engaged in a frenetic naval race. England viewed Germany's espousal of sea power as a threat to her very existence, as well as to her commerce and colonies. She girded herself to meet it and, in 1918, with the help of her allies (among them the United States), defeated Germany after four years of brutal war. Much the same scenario ensued in World War II, except that, if anything, the fighting at sea was more fierce. For her own reasons, Japan joined the Axis, initiated war by a well-planned surprise attack—and spread the modern armageddon to both oceans. While there was cause to hope the world could "get back to normal" after the Great War, it was clear there was no prospect of any such thing after the Second World War.

At the beginning of World War II, the airplane and the submarine, which had become viable nearly

Below: Aegis ships will carry the most sophisticated computers yet seen at sea. Their combat information center (CIC) and main-frame consoles were assembled on land for development and testing.

Facing: The "cruiser in the cornfield" is a replica of the bridge, antennas, radars and associated below-deck compartments of the USS Ticonderoga, our first such ship. Aegis, with improvements, will be the primary naval combat weapon system well into the twenty-first century. Only the computer can provide the split-second data evaluations required today.

26–27: *The F/A-18 Hornet has been called "a computer with wings." It is expected to be the most combat-worthy aircraft flying.*

28–29: *The Hornet's computerized cockpit. Instead of having to watch many round dials, pilots can call up readings as needed in a "heads up" display.*

simultaneously at the turn of the century, were set to change naval tactics forever. Henceforth, instead of being confined to the ocean's surface, navies would also be concerned with the air above it and the mysterious waters beneath. Speed and surprise, both particularly germane to the functions of navies, would have importance greater by an order of magnitude than before, since both airplane and submarine could attack with bewildering suddenness. But, although events were to prove the old ideas outmoded, not everyone accepted innovation. Something dramatic was needed to drive the point home to those who still thought only in terms of surface warfare, and World War II provided it from the start.

In World War I the German U-boat had made an indelible mark by nearly defeating England on the sea. Despite their small numbers and primitive weapons—at least by modern standards—the German submarines, commanded by daring skippers, actually controlled the sea for a time. It is now generally conceded that without the strenuous efforts made by England's allies, particularly the United States, the U-boats would have won the war by starving England of the vital materials she needed, including food. England fought back tenaciously, with all means available. Among these was an intensive effort to deprive U-boats of their principal weapon, submergence, by having them conform to cruiser rules of warfare. These required U-boats to surface to accost ships that seemed to be unarmed but did not curb British decoy ships. Germany's final abandonment of the restrictive rules was one of the causes of the United States' entry into the war.

The characterization of unrestricted submarine warfare as more unacceptable than other forms of warfare became so firmly fixed in public consciousness that it persisted into World War II. At the outset of that war, however, indiscriminate mass bombing by both sides led to the abandonment of the distinction—and within a year the World War I story was repeated. England was reeling from the German U-boat campaign when, in 1941, Churchill informed Roosevelt that the war was lost unless drastic action

Radiological contamination can result from a nuclear explosion in a ship's vicinity. Here a radiation-monitoring squad is holding a drill. Everyone in the squad must be completely covered. After inspecting actual "hot spots," men, and their coveralls, would undergo strict decontamination procedures.

could be taken, and immediately. The prime minister's appeal was soon answered. What is not well appreciated is the small size of the submarine force that compelled England's desperate plea. It began with some 57 U-boats, not all of them seagoing, and consisted of about 100 U-boats at the end of the first year of war. Of these, only about a third, with 1,500 men, could be on station at once. These few men had a groggy Great Britain on the ropes, ready for a knockout blow.

The aircraft story was different. At first, aircraft were used during World War I for observation behind the fighting fronts. After a few months "dogfights" began to take place, as well as a number of bombing raids. The exploits of these early fliers were romanticized by a public who, if it cried out against U-boat warfare, paid but little attention to the effects bombings had on victims. Flying was equated with progress, and therefore mass bombings were more acceptable. This attitude contributed to the development of aviation after World War I and to growing theories about air power; none of these, however, were enough to make the Allied navies truly air minded. Neither the impassioned arguments of zealous air power advocates, the increasing fury of the German bombing of Britain during the early stages of World War II, nor the demonstrated performance of carrier aircraft in maneuvers could cause the fundamental change in outlook that the situation demanded. In 1941 leaders of all navies still believed that the sea war would be won by a great, climactic clash of two opposing battle lines. Accepted roles for aircraft were scouting and "spotting" the fall of main battery shot. Aircraft carriers were big, vulnerable, useful to be sure, but too lightly armored to stand up against heavy gunfire. Since they would probably be used for detached raids, it was well always to know where the enemy carriers were; but the consensus was that when it came to the showdown, carriers would be relegated to the fringes.

Naturally, naval aviators thought otherwise. They continually demonstrated their concepts of new tactics as they visualized them; but the aviation advocates were too few in number, their stature was not yet great enough, and the facts were not yet clear. They even lost some ground in 1940, when the British carrier *Glorious* blundered on two German battleships and was sunk by gunfire. All the discussion and professional jealousy came to a devastating end, however, when the U.S. battle line was sunk at its moorings in Pearl Harbor by planes from Japanese carriers 230 miles away. Some fifty-six hours later, on 10 December (east longitude time), land-based Japanese planes sank the British *Prince of Wales* and *Repulse* at sea off Malaya. This effectively silenced any budding contention that results might have been different at Pearl Harbor had the fleet been alert and at sea, where it would have been if the attack had been anticipated. In retrospect, loss of the battleships, painful as it was, amounted to a net gain for the United States, because it demolished a whole line of outmoded thinking and catapulted the U.S. Navy into the age of three-dimensional war. The aircraft carrier, with a main battery able to engage in distant combat (as far as 400 miles), became Queen of Battles, replacing the battleship whose main battery guns ranged only 20 miles. The day of the battle line was irrefutably over. Nearly half a century later, the carrier is still queen. She and her escort ships form the carrier battle group, the operational unit at sea today, which is complemented by a huge expansion in the now-nuclear-powered submarine force.

Radar came into its own during the Second World War, when its value for early detection of approaching ships or aircraft first became apparent. Combining radar's ability to "see" a target with instant transmission of target data to defensive weapons—which themselves had to be kept in instant readiness—became mandatory. By the close of the war, radar had become an essential tool in guiding aircraft and antiaircraft weapons.

Toward the end of World War II, when kamikaze tactics put human brains into bombs, electronic fire control provided the only possible response. The desperate young fliers who believed sacrificial spirit and valor could make up for lack of material resources and triumph over steel-jacketed bullets were proved tragically wrong. The human cost to Japan was incalculable—and to no avail. Of the thousands of kamikazes, only a few hundred got through the fusilade and actually crashed into ships. Despite the stupendous sacrifice, no more than about 100 ships, most of them small, were sunk.

From this beginning, electronic warfare capabilities have advanced faster than those of any other technology. While nuclear energy has been harnessed for use in bombs, missiles and weapons of all kinds, to its unprecedented capability has been added the explosion in control and precision made possible by radar and microelectronics. This is where we are today, the custodians of an extraordinary combination of nuclear power and an ongoing revolution in electronic capabilities, one that may well prove the most significant of all the developments of human industry. One needs a little thought to appreciate the dimensions of our twentieth-century extension of the Industrial Revolution. In fact, a new term—the electronic-nuclear revolution—might be called for. Be that as it may, the effect on the U.S. Navy, and on all navies, of the powerful computer technologies and the staggering weaponry they control is incalculable.

At the beginning the United States was fortunate to lie beyond a sea so large that it was many months away from any danger. The sea was one of the benevolent factors that made possible the progressive idealism upon which our country was founded, and which is still so much a part of our national makeup. Today, however, the seas are a highway that can bring us sudden peril from any direction, and the world is full of jealousy for our success. The sea lets us act in our defense in ways that may be graduated from gentle to forceful, but to exercise this range of options we must remain technologically alert. *Keepers of the Sea* shows how the U.S. Navy views its mandate, gives some feeling for the sea and men of the sea, and presents some of the ships in which our officers and men, sailors all, serve today.

The ceremony of evening colors takes place wherever naval ships are in port. Four Spruance-*class destroyers, nested together in San Diego Bay, simultaneously lower their union jacks on the bow precisely when the colors come down aft. All is done, with pride, by the flag and whistle command of the senior ship present. When foreign warships are visiting, there is usually a band concert featuring their national anthems.*

services include the naval equivalents of a butcher shop, bakery, drugstore, laundry, dry-cleaning establishment, photo lab and print shop. There are barber shops, movies (shown in available spaces all over the ship), radio and TV stations, a post office, carpenter shop, weather bureau and library. A gymnasium is almost always improvised in a vacant compartment somewhere. Built-in conveyor systems for heavy equipment make it possible to move replacement jet engines quickly from their stowage to aircraft under repair in the hangar bay. There are escalators for heavily accoutered fliers and an elevator serving the island structure, which towers seventeen stories above the keel. The big carrier has everything it takes to be as self-sufficient as any city on land, including an airfield with special utilities and a completely equipped hangar that can be useful for other purposes, such as entertainment. Nevertheless, a carrier is not a city designed for comfortable living. She is a mobile airport, intended for one purpose only: to spread her umbrella over thousands of square miles of ocean and contiguous land, and there to carry out the mandate of the nation. Everything aboard is subordinate to that function.

If the U.S. Navy can be criticized for having been slow to emphasize naval air power before Pearl Harbor, it cannot be accused of failure to accept new ideas since then. The initial spur to innovation was the need to recover from Pearl Harbor's murderous insult, and the momentum has not slackened. For example, new and better ways of operating and maintaining ships have been adopted as fast as technology has revealed them. Nowadays, virtually all ship and aircraft operation and maintenance begin when a crewman scans a computer file of trouble-shooting procedures or replacement parts stored on "floppy" or "hard" disks, which are themselves located by reference to a master computer index of indexes. Upkeep of any large modern warship depends on several computer maintenance shops being connected with networks of data communication lines for mutual support. In battle, when it is crucial to repair damaged gear within minutes, critical spares can be located instantly. During a more leisurely paced

overhaul or refit, this efficiency pays off in another way: greatly reduced cost in time and money, which are always too short.

The current development in electronics, an explosion in technology without parallel in the history of the world, has also had an extraordinary effect on command, control and communications. If there is a critical factor that applies to all combat situations, it is having needed information readily available. Second in importance is the ability to make use of information by passing instructions rapidly to those who need them. Since the advent of radar, which, among other things, enabled ships to navigate in poor visibility, detect aircraft, avoid collision and control gunfire against fast-moving targets, the U.S. Navy has striven to be foremost in the use of electronics. Now most modern warships are floating computer complexes, the new big aircraft carriers, with their CICs, being among the most sophisticated. Automated electronic communication circuits (part of the navy tactical data system, or NTDS) exchange information instantaneously among the computer consoles of all ships in a battle group, giving its commander, in his carrier flagship, command control over a missile battery in a ship many miles away. In some installations, great wall panels take the place of the huge cathode-ray tubes more frequently associated with computer terminals. Such panels can monitor everything going on within a radius of several hundred miles. The naval leaders of World War II, who contended constantly with insufficient information and their inability to "get the word" accurately to subordinates, would be amazed at today's overflowing fulfillment of what they so desperately needed.

The vast amount of information that today's navy requires can be transmitted and received without even the delay occasioned by the necessity of speaking. An attacking missile can easily accomplish its mission in less time than it takes to send an emergency voice warning. To provide virtually instantaneous reaction to the high-speed threats of modern electronic warfare, the Aegis combat weapon system, which improves on NTDS, was developed. Briefly, the system consists of four fixed phased arrays, one covering each quadrant. Inputs are received by an intricate computer complex designed with high redundancy and self-correcting built-in programs. Aegis enables certain critically important command decisions to be transmitted, in code, in microseconds of real time. One stroke of a key can launch antimissile weapons against an enemy missile or aircraft, or set them on automatic, to be fired when the target being tracked reaches predetermined firing parameters.

Nor is this all. Modern electronic technology also keeps the battle group commander in minute-to-minute contact with the president and with the far-flung military staff system that connects him with all segments of our national defense. The National Command Authority, as this setup is called, is the mechanism by which the constitutional mandate for responsibility is exercised. Exactly how the national command works is not publicized, nor is the degree of detail a commander needs in his instructions before he reacts to a crisis at sea. The law establishing the position of top command is clear, however, for the weapons of today are too fearsome to allow any other course: the president has ultimate authority at all times over their use, and this responsibility he cannot delegate.

One arm of naval air power, land-based air, is independent of aircraft carriers, tailhooks and catapults. Naval shore-based aircraft include those used for cargo, training and various other special purposes, but most of these planes are the long-legged ASW (antisubmarine warfare) patrols, the P-3 Orions, employed in ocean surveillance, electronic reconnaissance and weather research. Carrying fifteen-man crews, fitted with magnetic detection equipment, storage and ejection facilities for many sonobuoys, computers for automatic tactical decisions, and mines, rockets and homing torpedoes for ASW, these aircraft can remain aloft half a day or more and cover more than 3,000 miles in one flight. They have four powerful turboprop engines, two of which

are normally used for patrol at slow speed, with the other two secured and feathered, ready for immediate restart if necessary. Through their command centers, the Orions are connected with the navy SOSUS system (the seabed sonar system that can detect and track submarines over vast ocean areas), and can thereby concentrate their efforts wherever enemy submarines are operating. Now fitted to launch the Harpoon missile, the P-3s also have an antiship strike capability.

The question of how aircraft carriers can be most effectively operated has become paramount, for among the massive changes wrought by nuclear power has been a return to the long sea-keeping capability of the days of sail. With conversion to steam, coal—then oil—became the arbiter of endurance at sea. Now, however, ships of war can once again stay at sea for extended periods of time. A nuclear task force consisting of the *Enterprise, Long Beach* and *Bainbridge* went around the world unsupported in 1964, conducting operations on its own or with friendly nations along the route. Our navy's Indian Ocean deployments have established new records for time on station. Several of our carriers have been deployed near the Persian Gulf for three quarters of a year at a time. Reactors can now be fueled for about thirteen years of steaming, and perfection of replenishment-at-sea techniques permits other ships to remain under way indefinitely as well. No one would think of reinstituting the privations seamen were accustomed to in the days of sail, but now that the old capability for sustained endurance at sea has been recovered, the navy's dependence on frequent port visits is being relegated to history. New at-sea records will be made, and some means must be found to requite the men who make them. More pay, though desirable, is not necessarily the answer. What is needed is further reinforcement of the private and personal satisfaction that, in the long run, is more important than anything else.

Another question is that of size, a perennial one for the big ships, be they battleships before World War II or aircraft carriers since. To keep things in proportion, it must be remembered that the large-deck carrier of today has nearly three times the displacement of the biggest battlewagon sunk at Pearl Harbor, nearly ten times the horsepower of its main engines, over half again its top speed and more than three times its complement. She is two-thirds again longer, has considerably more than double the maximum beam and, with her mobile air wing, can fight a battle at 400 miles instead of about 17. She costs more to build and operate than a smaller ship, needs more crew, more fuel and more ammunition. But she is tremendously more capable, for the potential of any ship, combat or merchant, varies exponentially with her size. By all odds, the large-deck aircraft carrier is today's measure of sea power.

The controversy over the size of warships has, of course, many facets; cost, vulnerability and capability are only some of the more prominent. Until recently, however, no one could point to actual war experience to bolster or counter any of the arguments about the performance of ships in the growing electronic environment—although Vietnam did indeed provide some strong insights. As might be expected, many of the participants felt, justifiably, that without firm roots in recent experience there was danger that the multilayered arguments being voiced were too much based on theory and emotion. So when the Falkland Islands conflict arose, they watched it carefully in order to give the discussion a more objective footing. Short and therefore easily studied, like our own Spanish-American War, it provides powerful object lessons in naval strategy.

The most obvious question raised by the Falklands Crisis concerns the capability of aircraft carriers and their planes. British carrier aircraft were too short in range and too few in number. Four important ships were sunk by bombs and two by missiles brought in, undetected, to extremely close range by surprisingly effective Argentine fliers. British casualties aboard ship included some 120 deaths and several times that number injured, a severe toll that might have been avoided had the aircraft carriers on the scene been able to maintain the long-range surveillance that is

doctrine in the U.S. Navy. Furthermore, the two small British carriers, which had no catapults, together could not field more than about a quarter of the combat planes one big American carrier could have flung into the air; and the planes that were launched had much less range, payload and endurance than catapulted fighters and attack aircraft would have had.

Anyone who looks into ship design will discover that the invariable price of an increase in function or capability is an increase in size. To get more speed, for example, a ship needs more power; this requires bigger boilers and engines, which in turn either expand the ship's dimensions or force a reduction in some capability, such as survivability under attack. If the price of greater speed turns out to be larger engines and boilers, the resulting size increase then requires yet another increment of engine power. On the other hand, if it is agreed that the size or cost of a ship must be reduced, a decision about which current capabilities will be given up or downgraded must be made. This is the nub of the argument about size. As the sea campaign for the Falkland Islands suggests, a compromise in quality is the mandate for either a compromise in outcome or an increase in the cost of success, which must be measured not only in treasure but in the lives of soldiers and sailors as well.

The U.S. Congress over the years has evidently agreed with the navy's arguments regarding the size and capabilities of aircraft carriers, since it has consistently appropriated the funds to continue building the "large decks." A proposal to make new ships about one third smaller lost when it was shown that at least two of the smaller carriers would have to be built to replace a single big one, and at a much larger overall cost. Pound for pound, the big carrier is by far the least costly ship of its type the navy can build. The proof lies in the way we have used these huge floating airfields in the past decades. It is through them that we have projected our sea power, and through them that we have carried out our national policies wherever, whenever, their impress was needed.

Pride in his work shows in this sailor's face. His brown shirt identifies him as a member of the all-volunteer flight deck crew. His status as plane captain, responsible for servicing "his" aircraft, is indicated by the chains, which are almost part of his uniform when they are not securing his plane to the ship.

Above: Predawn servicing of F-14 Tomcats. The great ship is at her quietest. On her starboard quarter, her birds are receiving fuel, air, hydraulic fluid and a general checkup. The plane captains are cleaning the Plexiglas canopies of their craft. Shortly, loudspeakers will bellow the order to clear the flight deck and, from that moment, organized chaos will reign as the flight deck crew and the aircraft begin their day's "ops."

Facing: Pilots are notoriously finicky about being able to see, and woe to the plane captain who does not turn over a spotless "bubble." The F-14's wings are swept back as though in high-speed flight. Each type of aircraft folds its wings in a different way—but folded they must be. Not until a plane is placed on the cat are its wings extended.

Above: A "FOD (foreign object damage) walk-down" is done before flight ops begin and from time to time thereafter. Anything loose on the flight deck can be lethal to a jet engine.

Right: A close-up of F-14s being serviced on the Eisenhower's *stern.*

A view of a carrier's navigation bridge, from which she is steered and commanded. Carriers have a second "bridge," primary flight control, for the direction of flight ops. In the foreground, a quartermaster and the OOD (officer-of-the-deck) are checking the chart.

Facing: Helicopters are useful in many ways. An SH-3 Sea King is in plane-guard station during flight ops, ready for water rescue in case of a mishap. Designed for ASW, the Sea King can carry electronic sensors, dipping sonar (a sonar it can "dunk" for submarine search) and other devices.

Below: The plane-guard helo is always the first launched and the last recovered, and must be relieved on station if flight ops outlast its endurance. Here an SH-3 is lifting off during flight ops. Steam from a catapult "shot" is still rising from No. 1 cat. An S-3 Viking is positioned for launch on No. 2 cat.

56–57: Second in normal launch sequence is the E-2C Hawkeye, a patrol plane with great endurance, a huge radar and continuous computer linkage to the carrier's CIC. Its radar disc is a distinctive feature. Several such planes are usually in the air at one time, providing continuous and precise radar coverage out to more than 300 miles. The time is daybreak.

Right: Looking aft (and into the tremendous tail-pipe of an A-7 Corsair) from the catwalk along the forward starboard side of the USS Independence's flight deck. Under the feet of the sailor on the right is No. 1 catapult, not in use at the moment.

Below: A carrier's primary flight control functions in much the same way as its civilian counterpart, but with more tension. The pri-fly tower resembles a ship's bridge, but instead of facing forward it faces the flight deck, its sole area of concern.

Right: In civilian airports this would be ground control. The pilot with two telephones directs the placement and movement of aircraft and people on the flight deck. Sometimes he is nearly as frantic as the air boss in pri-fly.

60–61: *A deck tractor is parking a Phantom, one of the navy's most successful all-weather multipurpose fighters. Beneath the plane's fuselage is a streamlined extra fuel tank. An F-4 can carry various missiles and bombs, including nuclear ones. The plane captain is in the pilot's seat, ready to apply the brakes.*

Above: An A-7 Corsair aboard the Independence *has just been "spotted" on the flight deck by one of the ship's low-slung tractors. Wheel chocks have been placed, and tie-down chains are about to be. The outboard bomb racks directly under the plane's folded wings have triple ejector racks to increase their loading.*

Right: The F-14 Tomcat will soon be launched. On the cat the pilot, his face mask in place and engines at full power, indicates readiness by saluting—at night, by turning on lights. The catapult officer, himself a pilot, touches the deck with hand or flashlight, then gives the launching signal by thrusting his body into a point.

Left: Something is not quite right with this F-14. The RIO (radar intercept officer) is checking his gear while the disgusted pilot registers impatience.

Below: The A-7 has just landed and taxied to a refueling station. Two "grapes" (refueling men in purple jerseys) hurry with a fuel hose. The plane can be refueled in minutes, a process directed by the air boss, and readied for immediate relaunch.

Bottom, facing: The A-6 Intruder is very versatile. This one is fitted with four external fuel tanks, two under each wing, and a pod containing the refueling drogue under the fuselage.

Left: Waiting his turn to taxi onto the cat, an F-14 pilot checks his fuel probe. He represents $300,000 in training; his plane is a multi-million-dollar investment.

65

Above: This Corsair leaves a visible path of jet exhaust as it roars off its catapult on a sunset practice mission.

Top: The catapult control station on a carrier's forecastle. Ear protectors are mandatory, and all orders must be given by hand signal. The officer's two upraised fingers indicate that his cat is in the final stages of preparation for launch. The green jersey's thumbs-up signal means steam settings are in order (note his private touch, a legless chair); the other two green jerseys, their jobs done, are required to sit or kneel. The other yellow jersey is probably an officer in training for the catapult.

Right: The flight deck viewed from aft. No. 3 waist cat has just fired; its steam shrouds the deck, and its jet blast deflector is already down for the next plane. A raised blast deflector obscures the plane on No. 4 cat.

Right: It takes two green-jersey equipment men to move the "box" that guides the launch bars of the aircraft onto the catapult shuttle.

Below: A Corsair, bellowing at full power, carrying five practice bombs and an extra fuel tank, is being hurled off the cat at 120–150 knots.

Right: Ordnance men load a general-purpose bomb onto a triple ejector rack under the wing of a Corsair.

Facing: Flight deck noise is overwhelming. Ear protectors allow shouting voices to come through, but they are not easy to hear in competition with slamming cats and roaring jets.

Facing: An emergency fire fighter on his truck. His flame protection gear allows him to dive through ignited fuel to rescue men from a burning plane.

Below: Crash emergency vehicles are usually painted red and white. Manned by specially trained crews, they stand by during all flight ops.

Bottom: This Intruder's catapult alignment was off by a few inches. Rather than have it taxi around again, the cat officer has ordered the plane shoved into line by hand.

72–73: *An F-14 crosses the blast deflector and engages its launch bar. Steam from the prior launch is still rising.*

74–75: *Rolling onto No. 1 cat, launch bar raised. Visible under the A-7's wing are a Sidewinder missile and a forward-looking infrared device. No. 2 cat's jet blast deflector is raised, indicating it has a plane ready.*

76–77: *A simultaneous launch from bow and waist cats. The carrier is not working to capacity, however, for No. 2 cat is obstructed.*

78–79: *Operational aircraft are nearly always flown off carriers prior to entry into port. These F-14s from the USS Eisenhower are making a high-speed pass over* home base after a long deployment. Their top speed is above mach 2, ceiling 60,000 feet.

Above: One of the USS Nimitz's Tomcats test-fires a Phoenix missile. It has at least one other tucked beneath its fuselage. The Phoenix missile system can engage six targets at one and the same time. In 1981 two Tomcats shooting older Sidewinder missiles returned the fire of two Libyan jets and destroyed them.

Facing: The No. 2 man in an F-14 Tomcat. Some modern naval aircraft have more capability than one man can handle. The Tomcat, a 35-ton "air superiority fighter," is designed for a two-man crew: a pilot and a radar intercept officer. Among other duties, the latter navigates, operates radar systems and fires missiles.

82–83: *A "fleur-de-lis" executed by the Blue Angels. Their A-4s are maintained at the peak of condition, with throttle settings and control surfaces calibrated for exact station keeping. The smoke is, of course, meant to make their coordinated maneuvers visible, but everything they demonstrate, including formation* *flying, is a standard part of combat training. Their precision is invariably thrilling.*

Facing and below: In the CIC. This group of compartments is off limits to many crewmen because of the presence of exposed classified information. All aircraft, ships and missiles are plotted automatically and by hand, as shown at left, for instant reference. Information arrives continuously from a variety of sensors, including those in far-off E-2C Hawkeyes and SH-3 Sea King helicopters. Some of these consoles can launch weapons and take defensive countermeasures at the stroke of a key.

86–87: *With tailhook down, a Phantom comes in at sunset. Four wires are stretched out on the carrier's flight deck, and the plane will try to catch the third. The instant he feels his wheels touch the deck, the pilot will apply full throttle. If the restraining harness does not almost immediately dig into his belly and shoulders, indicating that the arresting gear has engaged, he knows the hook failed to catch a wire. In that event he flies off the runway, his dragging hook leaving behind a shower of sparks.*

Below: An aircraft on the glide path is narrowly watched by two landing signal officers. Tension is rising because the landing area is not clear. They hold aloft the "wave-off" and "add power" light switches to show pri-fly that they are about to send the plane back around the landing pattern.

Bottom: Just before touchdown. In contrast to civilian aircraft landing on a long runway, carrier aircraft land in a tail-down attitude. They come in at about 75 percent power, in what has been termed a controlled crash, and immediately on impact go to full power, ready to take off if their hook fails to grab a wire. The

planes guide themselves in by keeping the mirrored reflection of a large orange ball between rows of vertical and horizontal lights. In the face of wave-off lights, however, aircraft may not land, even in an emergency.

Above: At 120 knots, a Tomcat has hit the deck with 70 to 80 tons of impact, grabbed a wire and, in two seconds, stopped. A director is signaling the pilot to cut power so the arresting gear's "pullback" will disengage the tailhook.

90–91: *The springlike pullback of the arresting cable has got this Corsair rolling gently backward, but not enough to have disengaged the hook when the wire slackened. The equipment man is signaling for another yank backward. If that fails members of the deck crew will rush forward and unhook by hand. Speed is essential, for another plane is already on the ball in the landing approach, and this one must taxi clear at once.*

92–93: *Fliers being debriefed in the intelligence center show fatigue. Experienced debriefing officers extract needed information mercifully and quickly.*

Above: Guantánamo Bay is a magnificent harbor bordering an ideal training and operating area. Most U.S. Navy ships train here sometime during their careers. The heat can be oppressive, setting the stage for such spectacular photographs as this one, which shows both sides of the hangar deck open for ventilation.

The space between the top of the hangar and the bottom side of the armored flight deck is used for living and working compartments.

Left: Aircraft elevators are on the sides of new carriers instead of in the middle of their flight decks, as in earlier designs. The result is more useful deck space on both hangar and flight decks. Here two planes are being lowered to the hangar deck.

Facing: Nearly every skill known to man is needed by the navy. This electronics technician has one of the most valuable. With the best test equipment now available, he can spot problems and make repairs unheard of a few years ago. Here, he is analyzing a malfunctioning panel.

Below: A large-deck carrier has a hangar the size of a dozen tennis courts, in which some 30 planes, plus boats, cranes, tractors and gear of all kinds, can be stowed and serviced. At sea or in port, engines can be replaced, structural repairs can be made, and hydraulic, air and electrical systems can be reworked.

Bottom: To function at all, an aircraft carrier has to have a complex and efficient spare parts system. A computerized index and inventory, shown here, make it all possible.

98–99: *A time shot at night of a ghostly bow. Moving lights appear as streaks. The Corsair dips as it is fired off No. 1 cat, then rises as flying speed increases. To its left, cat crewmen wait for the aircraft moving up to No. 2. The pulsating red light in the upper left is from a plane going around again.*

Surface Combatants:

Traditional Guardians of the Sea

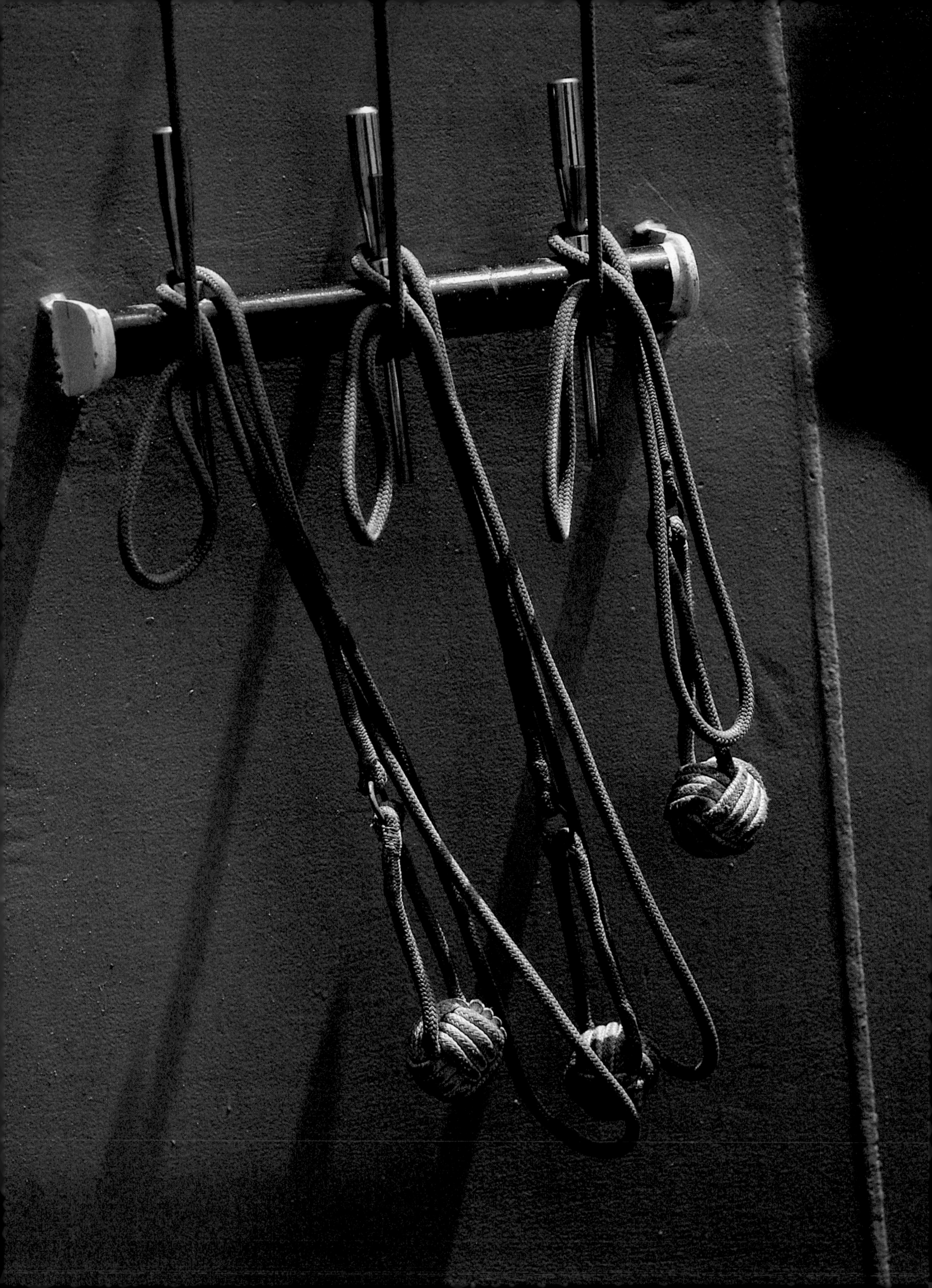

It is 0800 on an overcast morning at sea. A rapid bonging sounds over the internal communications speakers throughout a solitary haze-gray warship. An urgent announcement follows: "General quarters! All hands man your battle stations for live firing exercise!" On board the *Spruance*-class destroyer, steaming beyond sight of the capital ship she is screening some 30 miles distant, seamen and officers alike scramble to their assigned fighting stations. However, unlike their counterparts in similar circumstances in the bygone destroyers of World War II, her gunners mates head, not for her two 5-inch dual-purpose gun mounts, but for a gun and missile fire control computer complex deep inside the ship. Her commanding officer, rather than take his traditional position on the ship's bridge, proceeds to a computer-driven display console in the CIC within the superstructure. And her engineers, instead of spreading throughout her main engineering spaces, gather in the main control room where operation of the ship's propulsion is monitored and controlled by remote means. For in the U.S. Navy of the 1980s, a destroyer's guns are fully automated, and need not be loaded, fired or even manned by gunners mates; her main batteries are sophisticated electronically guided missiles; her remote-control gas-turbine jet engines and controllable-pitch propellers drive her effortlessly through the water at speeds that range from zero to 30 plus knots, or can shift her from flank ahead to full astern in less than a minute; and her commanding officer's battle station is located where the eyes and ears of the ship—her radar arrays and powerful SQS–53 sonar—can present their target data to him instantaneously and completely.

During the centuries before the advent of submarines and naval aircraft, control of the sea depended solely on surface ships. Whether warships were driven by sail or steam, made of wood or steel, the basic principles of sea power remained essentially the same. But all that changed in the first half of the twentieth century. The German U-boats in World War I were first to demonstrate that sea power no longer resided only on the surface; the attack on Pearl Harbor and other key Pacific battles proved that naval air forces could be no less devastating. The effectiveness of air and submarine warfare in World War II marked the demise of the surface battle line, and the prospects of nuclear war in the late forties and in the fifties supported this evaluation. However, the Korean War and other Cold War crises soon indicated that not all future conflicts would be nuclear, and that many tasks beyond the capabilities of aircraft and submarines would still have to be performed. The problem confronting naval planners in the sixties and seventies was to define what these missions might be and how best to carry them out in the face of the twin considerations of economy and rapidly expanding technology.

As the decade of the seventies opened, most surface combatant ships were hybrids whose main batteries consisted of one or more of three basic types of guided missiles, some guns of various sizes and a mix of fire control systems. In their time these ships served their purpose, providing the means not only for ready defense but for testing newly developed weapons as well. However, the need for an entirely new sort of surface warship, born of the latest advances in technology and geared to the updated tenets of naval strategy, was clear. The science of electronics was developing so rapidly that new weapons were obsolescent before they could be put in service. Even the bigger warships of World War II could not readily be modified to fit the new requirements. Surface warships built after the war were fine ships and performed well in the fifties and sixties; essentially, however, they were no more than extensions of wartime designs. Ships that could keep pace with the new era for a full twenty-year span of operational life and longer were needed.

The *Spruance*-class destroyer is the first operational class of surface warships expressly developed to meet the requirements of sea warfare in the eighties and beyond. She has emerged from over twenty years of debate that reverberated in the Pentagon, in the media, and in the halls of Congress over the proper role of the surface warship. Her basic design

Preceding: The USS Ticonderoga, *built basically on a* Spruance *hull and equipped with the sophisticated Aegis combat weapon system, is one of the most thoroughly tested ships our navy has ever commissioned. During builder's trials her missiles and guns were fired many times, her control and maneuverability checked in all possible ways. She is shown launching a Standard missile, her potential dramatically outlined in reduced visibility. The muzzle of one of her automatic 5-inch guns shows forward of the obscured missile launcher.*

Facing: A signalman's pride. These halyards on a flagship's bridge are specially belayed for quick release to hoist the signal flags rapidly. The halyards are led through rings above; the "monkey fists" on the halyard ends keep them from passing through the rings and going adrift during the flurry of getting up a signal.

will be fundamental to our navy's surface ship program well into the twenty-first century. To begin with, the *Spruances* are big ships, over 8,000 tons, as opposed to a typical World War II destroyer's 2,800 tons or the 1,100 tons of a World War I four-piper. Their 563-foot length is comparable to that of many World War II light cruisers. Yet, thanks to maximum automation, they carry considerably smaller crews. Their endurance is over 6,000 nautical miles at 20 knots. In theory, their engine rooms need not be manned, even though ship's speed may be well over 30 knots on her four gas turbines. Under almost all conditions, and merely by pressing starter buttons, engines are ready for full operation in two minutes.

Designed primarily for antisubmarine escort duty with a carrier battle group, *Spruances* are carefully engineered for noise reduction. In addition to their two dual-purpose 5-inch guns, they have short-range antiaircraft missiles and automatic Gatling guns, Harpoon antiship missiles, Asroc (antisubmarine rockets tipped with homing torpedoes or atomic depth charges), two triple antisubmarine warfare (ASW) torpedo launchers, and hangar space for two LAMPS III submarine-hunting helicopters. The ships are so commodious that they have been facetiously described as yachts masquerading as warships. The fact is that to allow for the fast-moving changes in all categories of electronic science, they have a great deal of space set aside for anticipated new equipment. Indeed, the four *Kidd* variants of the class have already been given full antiair warfare (AAW) suits in addition to the ASW abilities built into the original *Spruance* design: their short-range AAW missiles have been replaced by a pair of twin launchers for the Standard medium-range antiaircraft missile. All *Spruances* are a mass of computers and electronics; everything, from the CIC to the main engines, is run by computers and other electronic circuitry. Their masts bristle with antennas. Sonars and radars, linked directly to digital computers by hundreds of intricate miles of cables, process data with lightning speed.

In no other class of ship has the economic potential of mass production been so exploited. All *Spruances*, to date more than thirty, have been built in the same shipyard to reduce costs and construction time. The advantages of this are offset by the disadvantage of concentrating jobs and know-how in a single place. For later destroyers, such as the planned *Arleigh Burke* (DDG 51) class of some sixty ships, which will also carry the Aegis combat weapon system, the standard practice of competitive bidding for portions of the construction program will be followed.

The soundness of the *Spruance* concept is probably best demonstrated by the new gas-turbine-powered Aegis cruiser *Ticonderoga* (CG 47), which was completed at Pascagoula, Mississippi. She is the first of several ships designed from the beginning to incorporate the Aegis system. From keel to main deck, she is virtually identical to her *Spruance* relatives. She carries all the same weapons as a *Kidd*-class destroyer, although above her main deck she differs notably in appearance. Like the *Spruance*, she has two automatic 5-inch guns. Like a *Kidd*, she also has a pair of twin trainable launchers for the Standard missile. Later ships will forgo these launchers in favor of the VLS (vertical launch system), which can fire three or four types of missiles directly out of launch openings in the main deck. The *Ticonderoga* carries Harpoon cruise missiles as well as Asroc. These weapons, along with the long-range Tomahawk cruise missiles to be added later, can be launched from the same VLS. For close-in defense against missiles that have somehow evaded all other countermeasures, the *Ticonderoga* has two Phalanx multi-barrel 20-mm Gatling guns that can fire their rounds at a phenomenally high rate; a computerized radar and fire control system initiates fire automatically when a target comes within range. She also has all of the *Spruance*'s ASW capability, including her powerful sonar. The *Ticonderoga*'s combined fire control system and search radar, featuring four Aegis fixed arrays, are, however, totally different. Her detecting radar, fire control radar and weapons systems—and all their associated computers—are integrated into a single system that can be set up for automatic operation. The fore part of the ship is one big computer complex, designed for the easy replacement of failed components. (A computer buff would be in heaven working with the 792,000 thirty-two-bit words of base programming, the seventeen UYK-7 computers, the 3.5 megawords overall in the ship.) The Aegis system allows a single ship to track hundreds of targets and aim, fire and guide her weapons to engage them all within seconds of first contact.

Present navy programs call for the construction of twenty-four Ticonderoga-class ships. They will be key elements of all battle groups. The Ticonderogas are the ideal flagships for AAW commanders, better equipped than any other ships to maintain a precision data base of everything going on in the air, on the surface and under it, and to react fast to all threats. They can direct a defensive missile to be fired from the magazine of an accompanying ship and send it aloft to destroy an attacking missile or aircraft. These ships will also play major roles in antisurface warfare and ASW. They are acknowledged as the most completely integrated, computerized combat systems yet developed, a milestone that bids fair to redress the unfavorable balance of power with which surface warships have been plagued for so many years. The navy has put the computer to sea with an emphasis never before seen. Even without a war to prove themselves, the Ticonderoga and her sisters will revolutionize control of the sea.

A special category of surface warships merits particular notice: the nuclear-powered cruisers. These handsome ships are marginally larger than the Kidds and Ticonderogas and, except for the much larger Long Beach, are similarly armed. In due course, some may have their radar and electronics suits converted to an Aegis-type system. These are, of course, expensive ships, but their nuclear-powered engines have been extremely successful, not only because of their great cruising range and high reliability but also because the elimination of fuel requirements extends all other battle group capabilities. The ideal carrier battle group is the all-nuclear one, since no ship propulsion fuel need be carried or brought to it. The navy wants four nuclear-powered carrier battle

groups, two based in the Atlantic and two in the Pacific, for quick response to National Command Authority orders in emergencies. Each nucleus will be augmented by the long-range, gas-turbine-powered Spruances, Ticonderogas and Burkes when conditions demand.

The significant fact about cruisers, destroyers and frigates in service today is that, no matter what their classification, all are actually different versions of the same type: the destroyer. We have nuclear- and conventionally powered cruisers, long-range conventionally powered destroyers and a large number of single-screw "economy" frigates. All these ships, designed for escort duties, are equipped with the most modern electronics for radar, sonar and fire control, and are armed principally with missiles. Some, the nuclear cruisers and large destroyers, were given the speed, endurance, weapons and computers to enable their operation with centralized combat command in carrier battle groups or surface action groups. Older destroyers, which can still render excellent account of themselves in AAW, are used more often for ASW screens. The frigates, also equipped with missiles and computers, are smaller and less expensive by far. They are intended for escort of amphibious battle groups or other task forces requiring less range and speed than the primary carrier battle groups. They will also perform convoy duty should a future naval war require it. The newest ships of all three types were designed for mass production, small crews, highly advanced electronic capabilities and a large reserve for the addition of new or upgraded equipment. All were conceived from the start to be quality vessels.

It was in the past that the navy maintained a clear distinction between the various kinds of surface ships. Destroyers began life before the turn of the century as "torpedo boat destroyers"—because of their thin hulls, affectionately referred to as tin cans, a name they still retain—whose specific mission was to accompany and protect the battle fleet against tiny warships armed with the automobile (self-propelled) torpedo. Within a few years the torpedo boat func-

106–107: *A frigate of the* Knox *class, supporting amphibious exercises off Coronado, California, is silhouetted against the sunset. Forty-six Knox-class ships were built in the sixties and seventies. Designed for ASW, they carry a variety of weapons and a crew of 220 and, until the completion of the more numerous Perry-class,* *were the largest post-war class of U.S. surface combatants.*

tions were absorbed by the larger, more proficient destroyers. As the role of battleships expanded from purely coastal defense to include sea control, the primary mission of destroyers, which escorted the battle fleet wherever it went, was extended as well. Combining the speed to catch torpedo boats with the guns to overpower them, these efficient little ships also supplanted the much older seagoing gunboats. Destroyers rapidly grew in size as improved technology gave them greater range, higher speed and better sea-keeping ability. Shallow-water river gunboats aside, by mid-century destroyers could perform all the functions of surface warships except carry aircraft and battle with big guns. The latter was still the province of the cruisers and battleships.

With destroyers at one end of the spectrum and battleships at the other, the cruisers held the middle ground. For a time they were known as the eyes of the fleet, a reference to their scouting mission in fleet actions. Over the years there have been many different cruiser types, reflecting the disparate constraints that influenced their designs. Such terms as *scout cruiser, protected cruiser, third-class cruiser, armored cruiser, light cruiser, heavy cruiser, county cruiser, treaty cruiser* and *battle cruiser* have had their day. All these types were originally designed to have an armor and armament advantage over smaller ships with higher speed and a speed advantage over larger ships with more powerful guns. But the survivability of cruisers was threatened in World War II when the speed of battleships, approaching the theoretical maximum for displacement hulls, began to rival theirs. During the war and for a time afterward, "heavy" and "light" cruisers differed solely in the size of their main battery guns; some of the "lights" were actually bigger ships than some of the "heavies." Even these distinctions vanished when missiles began to supplant guns.

Today, none of the older missile cruisers converted from wartime cruisers remain in service. Destroyers, meanwhile, have continued to grow in size to the point where some of them have been redesignated cruisers. The *Bainbridge* and the *Truxtun*, the first

nuclear destroyers, were reclassified as cruisers after a decade's service. All the nuclear surface escorts built after them are now called cruisers. In reality such designations are now meaningless. All surface fighting ships are grouped into a single category. The battle line disappeared in one day of madness and so did the time-honored functions associated with it. Today all surface warships, from frigate to battleship, may be utilized as battle group or convoy escorts, in AAW or ASW roles, for shore bombardment in support of amphibious operations, or independently.

The name *frigate* has been excessively bandied about. In the mid-fifties we tried to resurrect our historical love affair with the frigates of 1812 by upgrading the term to refer to the larger destroyers of post–World War II vintage. Foreign navies not following suit, we gave up the effort after a few years. The term now refers to small, moderate speed, lightly armed escort ships, fitted principally for ASW and to a lesser degree for AAW. Frigates are intended for all escort and convoy tasks, except those associated with carrier battle groups and surface action groups. For economy's sake they have only one propeller; early classes have steam turbines, while the latest are propelled by gas turbines. Since World War II they have been built in great numbers, as the *Knox* class of forty-six ships shows. The later *Oliver Hazard Perry* class of guided-missile frigates will include more than fifty units. One of this class, the *McInerney*, has been modified for experimentation with the LAMPS III, the sub-hunting helicopter that can operate as far as 100 miles from its mother ship and still remain in computer contact with her. LAMPS III will eventually go aboard most new surface ships and be back-fitted to many older ones. When the helicopter is fully operational, a single *McInerney* or *Spruance* will be able to maintain surveillance over hundreds of square miles of ocean, locate enemy submarines without revealing her presence, and attack them with lethal accuracy.

Neither the destroyer nor the cruiser nor the frigate, despite their sophisticated equipment, is built to withstand the sort of attack launched with modern weapons. Their lack of armor disturbs naval leaders concerned that ships in combat will be the targets of highly accurate, electronically guided missiles. Defense of most of the U.S. Navy's surface ships is entirely preventive: it depends on intercepting missiles before they can reach their targets. Only our aircraft carriers and the fast battleships being returned to service are what might be termed hardened, that is, able to take punishment as well as dish it out. The *New Jersey*'s armor, designed to protect the ship's vitals against 16-inch armor-piercing shells, should be equally effective against missiles with conventional high-explosive warheads.

Hardened design for surface ships is only one of the lessons gleaned from the Falkland Islands Crisis. Further evaluation will probably come down in favor of greatly improved protection, massive electronic capability, high endurance, high speed and a flexible repertoire of operational capabilities. In addition, it will be recommended that ships be more densely loaded with weapons than has been the case since 1945; these will include great numbers of long-range surface-to-surface, surface-to-air and ASW missiles. To the U.S. Navy's credit, most of these considerations had been incorporated in the design for the *New Jersey*'s rehabilitation before the Falkland Islands confrontation took place. More changes undoubtedly will come. In her final configuration, the *New Jersey* might lose her after turret and gain a short flight deck. She will carry many different missiles with sophisticated electronic and computer controls. Her extraordinarily thick armor would have barely shrugged at the impact of the Exocet missile that put the British destroyer *Sheffield* out of action in the Falkland Islands. The addition of a flight deck and of surface-to-surface, air-breathing Tomahawk cruise missiles, whose range is several hundred miles, together with her remaining 16-inch main battery guns, will make the *New Jersey* an extremely versatile ship.

The computer age is still far too new for its effect on the men of the navy to be conclusively evaluated. Some people think that it may produce a new breed of sailor, perhaps some sort of computer-seaman. Such sailors would be as familiar with the words and chips of computers as traditional seamen are with the anchor-windlass gear on the forecastle or boat handling in a seaway. Crew sizes are coming down, professionalism and individual responsibility are on the rise. More of the routine upkeep will have to be accomplished in port by shore-based workers, for the old navy of paint, polish and personnel inspection on Saturdays is giving way to weekend liberty and working inspections under way. No longer does a ship enter port and put hundreds of men over the side to paint her—not when most of her crew are technicians exempt from the time-honored sailors' chores of paint, polish and scrub. At home base others will increasingly have to take over, so that crew members, like their ship or aircraft, can replenish body and soul. Already there are no slack days. Ships today are like aircraft or thoroughbred racehorses: highly stressed, powerful beyond imagining. Their crews must be performers extraordinaire.

In the old days, ships lay in harbor between cruises much longer than the hard-driven ships of today do. Periods of "miscellaneous at anchor," when operations were suspended for routine cleaning and maintenance, were frequently scheduled. Such leisure is unheard of nowadays. Ships are better built and more functional than ever before, and their capabilities and importance to defense are such that the national interest pushes them unmercifully. It is not uncommon for modern warships to log three, four and five times as many miles and hours under way as their predecessors did in the years before World War II. More time at sea requires greater dedication from the crew, and the resulting personal sacrifice must be requited in some way. More than twenty years ago the problem was faced squarely in the ballistic missile submarine program, with the result that each such submarine has ever since had two separate crews, a blue and a gold, which take alternate patrols. No other navy ships have two crews.

For a time many believed that the airplane had spelled the death of the surface warship, since Pearl

Harbor and the loss of the *Prince of Wales* and the *Repulse* appeared to prove that ships confined to the surface of the sea could not fight back against the lethal wasps of enemy air. This was true enough for 1941, but the terrible affliction of the fleet at Pearl Harbor lay more in its lack of adequate weapons than in any inherent superiority of a flying machine over a floating one. At last clearly aware of what air power could do to sitting ducks unable to fight back, the U.S. Navy quickly began to act. It had to, of course, or surface warships would never go to sea again; but go to sea they did, their decks literally covered with new AAW gun emplacements and the radar sets to achieve adequate aim. Sheer brute force was the answer to planes of that time, for they were required to come in close for strafing and dive-bombing or the self-immolation of a kamikaze attack. Millions of bullets made the close-in aircraft attack less than likely to succeed. The kamikazes, for the most part idealistic youths who had had no time for training in the fine points of combat flying, discovered that getting through that cloud of angry lead was not easy, no matter how fervid their determination.

But this, of course, was only an interim answer, one geared to the desperation of the war years, and it led to the next stage in the contest between surface combatants and aircraft. For the latter, the solution was a weapon that could be fired at long range with a good chance of hitting—in other words, with some kind of terminal guidance. After the war, missile technology developed rapidly, as did homing devices, and again the balance swung in favor of aircraft and missiles. Cruise missile development by the Soviets suddenly turned heads. In the sixties they were reported to have developed something that could fly at high speed only feet above the water's surface (thus remaining immune to radar detection) for more than 100 miles, and then home in on and attack the biggest target within the acquisition range of its sensors. To this weapon, at least theoretically, all surface ships, even carriers, were vulnerable, especially in the nuclear war that some people feared was imminent. The successful missile attacks on British ships during the Falkland Islands hostilities seemed to verify the superiority of the cruise missile. But the balance continued to swing, albeit not in time to be tested in that dispute.

Interestingly enough, the electronically guided missile has confirmed the survival, rather than marked the end, of the surface man-of-war. Missiles are not as easy to install in aircraft as in ships, which have the added advantage of being able to carry far greater numbers of weapons. Moreover, heavy armor, which was deemed useless for ships doomed to sink from a single atomic blast, has now been recognized as an effective means of protection against nonnuclear missiles that get through sequential rings of defense. If it is probable that future battle will take place beneath the nuclear threshold, an able force on the sea is essential to the defense of the United States. Even in the case of nuclear war, far better for it to be fought at sea than on land.

The computer explosion, which threatened to make a sure and devastating hit out of almost every weapon fired, for a time had people quaking at the thought of homing weapons. But most nonnuclear missiles do not have the armor-piercing capabilities of a plunging 16-inch shell, and against the armored vitals of properly hardened ships can do only minor damage. In the meantime, computers and radar technology can benefit ships as well as aircraft, and ships can always carry more different types of equipment, and provide more power to operate it, than aircraft can. Lo and behold, ships can now shoot back at aircraft at extremely long ranges and with increasing chance of success. Opposed by a properly functioning Aegis system, in short, no airplane has much of a chance of reaching missile launch position. Similarly, pitted against modern sonar, able to detect passively or actively out to three convergence zones, the most modern submarine will have great difficulty getting to attack position undiscovered. Missiles launched by either airplane or submarine will have to run the gamut of the most sophisticated missile defense system yet conceived. The centuries-old contest between offense and defense continues, and the balance, for now, is being restored.

Receiving a foreign officer on board is still a formal occasion in certain circumstances. Here, during a joint exercise, a senior Royal Navy task group commander comes aboard the U.S. flagship "by wire." He wears a white uniform under his flight clothes and will resume his dignity after shedding the coveralls.

Above, left: Officers' call on a pleasant morning in the Pacific. The executive officer (back to camera) discusses the ship's plan of the day. Working uniforms at sea lean to practicality and comfort.

Left: The forecastle of the USS Richmond K. Turner, *a guided-missile cruiser. She has two anchors, one to starboard and one centered on her stem. The windlass of the latter is in the foreground. The proper handling of anchor gear is a matter of pride.*

Above: A nest of three Spruance-class destroyers at the San Diego Naval Base. Like the Richmond K. Turner, *they have no port anchor. The extreme rake of their bows prevents their anchors from striking the big bow-mounted sonar dome. The anchors weigh about half a ton each. Bicycles in the rack on the pier belong to crew members, who may keep "civvies" on board and, if authorized, wear them when they go on liberty.*

114–15: *The return of the battleship does not herald the return of the battle line, but the recommissioned* New Jersey's *rapier-like 16-inch guns still have the old bravura of brute power as she steams westward into the Pacific.*

Facing: An OOD on the destroyer Harry W. Hill *takes the bearing of another ship. A skipper must have full confidence in his OODs because the safety of his ship and crew, and his own future career, may depend on their good judgment. To qualify as an OOD, an officer has to pass exacting tests.*

Below: The plotting table in a destroyer's CIC. The officer wears a telephone headset for instant communication with the OOD and the captain.

Bottom: The destroyers Barney *and* Charles F. Adams *break away from column formation and head out for their screening stations.*

118–19: *The climate-conditioned main engine control room of a* Spruance-class *destroyer. The engineering officer of the watch, left, has an overview of all turbine control panels and operators. The ship can make more than 30 knots on her four 20,000-hp gas turbines, which are con-trolled and monitored in much the same way as the aircraft jet engines from which they were developed.*

Above: Submarines used to be feared because of the torpedoes they fired, but the tables have turned. Now submariners fear a homing torpedo more than any other antisubmarine device, for a submerged sub cannot tolerate even a small hole in her pressure hull. This new Spruance-class destroyer has two triple launchers

for deadly acoustic-homing ASW torpedoes.

Top, facing: All ships need machine shops for small or emergency repairs. The latest ships of the U.S. Navy have highly capable repair facilities.

Bottom, facing: Humor can go a long way in the closed community of a ship on a long cruise.

Wise skippers condone a reasonable amount of it, and sometimes even initiate it themselves. The sailor is painting a sign on the door to one of the ship's magazines.

122–23: All work and no play makes Jack a dull boy. However, keeping up his game probably costs this sailor a few dollars, for aboard ship there is nothing analogous to "man overboard" for lost tennis balls. Exercise at sea is always a problem, which many modern ships try to solve by improvising gyms in empty compartments. The "tennis court" here is a helicopter landing area.

Above: Crew's quarters in new ships are a far cry from those in old ones. Each bunk has its own reading light, ventilation, built-in locker and privacy curtain. Civvies and certain other uniform items are stowed in the upright lockers on the left.

Far right: An officers' wardroom is dining room, classroom, living room and movie theatre. In small ships, the captain (far end) messes with his officers. In large ones, he takes his meals in private but often invites guests. The red jacket of the mess management specialist (serving) is this wardroom's touch of class.

Right: Spruances, designed with extra room to accommodate future needs, often put their presently unused spaces to good use for their crews. This gymnasium was built and equipped with money from the ship's welfare and recreation fund.

126–27: *Three nuclear cruisers in close proximity at Newport News Shipyard. The USS* Arkansas, *in the foreground, is transferring a missile to the* Mississippi, *alongside to port. The* Texas *is on the far side of the pier. In the background is the conventionally powered amphibious command ship* Mount Whitney.

Facing: At maximum elevation, one of the New Jersey's guns can speak with authority in support of an amphibious landing 20 miles away. A properly equipped battleship, possessed of sufficient speed and able to withstand heavy punishment, is the best escort an aircraft carrier can have.

Right: This gun director with its radar dish controls the fire of the ship's 5-inch 54-caliber gun. The helmeted officer with binoculars is a safety observer during target practice.

Right: Hatches, or access openings that are "dogged down" at battle stations, sometimes have small scuttles for emergency passage. Following a drill, this member of a damage control team emerges from a scuttle, a miner's lamp on his helmet and his oxygen mask, just removed, in hand.

Right: In a high-threat environment, two older destroyers will team up to double the firing rate. The Standard missile now has a range of about 25 miles—with booster, nearly 100.

Below: The bridge telephone talker at battle stations is a vital link in ship communications.

Right: A Harpoon surface-to-surface missile is launched port side forward. The control radar for the after missile launcher, with a white dot in its center, is in the upper right corner.

Left: A Standard missile with booster leaves a forward launcher of the USS Richmond K. Turner. *The booster will drop off in flight.*

Facing: Target drones, or unmanned remote-control planes such as the one being retrieved here, are expensive and should be recovered, if possible. In proof tests involving live warheads, however, some are deliberately hit and destroyed.

Right: Semaphore is an art still practiced by all signalmen. It is slow but, like flashing light, it is not susceptible to electronic interference or interception.

134–35: *It is nearly sunset at Norfolk Naval Base. Absentee pennants flying at port yardarms indicate that the skippers of these three combatants are ashore. The square indentations of the hull plating result from years of pounding by the sea. The USS Biddle, right, an 8,000-ton guided-missile cruiser, has her anchor lowered for painting. A sister ship, identical except for the radar on her mainmast, is inboard, moored alongside the pier. The third ship, left, is a much-altered World War II destroyer.*

Below: A pilot in a LAMPS III helo. His task is not only to fly his chopper but also to lay sonobuoys in a programmed pattern. He has a copilot and two systems operators. His torpedoes can be fired either by computer from the mother ship or by his own computer.

Facing: A LAMPS III helicopter is dropping a sonobuoy as part of a submarine detection exercise. Signals from distant buoys permit both helo and mother ship to track submarines.

Right: The panel in the side of this LAMPS III helo is loaded with sonobuoys ready for ejection. These devices transmit acoustic data via radio to ships or planes nearby. Some sonobuoys listen passively for submarine sounds; they emit neither noise nor signal and thus escape detection by submarines.

Above, left: The guided-missile frigate McInerney *patrols with her main weapons system in operational status. Her 10-ton Lamps III helo may be 100 miles away, tracking a target. Her extended stern handles her helo, and her specially configured CIC remotely tracks and lays weapons on a detected submarine.*

Left: The McInerney's *skipper and ASW officer make action decisons in the CIC with the help of their computer display. The CIC is the captain's battle station.*

Above: A LAMPS III helo can be recovered in 15-foot seas, when the ship is rolling 30 degrees and wind velocity is 25 knots. The helo drops a messenger line and hauls up a wire cable before being hydraulically winched down against the lift of the rotor blades. When its wheels touch the deck, the helo is "trapped" by massive jaws that clamp on a steel probe. The rotors are folded and the clenched jaws, on tracks, drag the bird into its hangar bay.

Submarines:
Prowlers
of the Deep

Somewhere south of Iceland the USS *Midwest City*, a relatively new nuclear attack submarine of the powerful and fast *Los Angeles* class, is on patrol. Her skipper has imposed the most stringent silencing measures upon watchstanders and men off duty. He could not give them the information received in a special top-secret briefing just before leaving port, but in the closely knit crew of a submarine, danger is easily sensed. The *Midwest City* has consciously converted herself into a submerged intelligence center. No errant sound in the ocean has escaped her notice; not a single detectable noise has emanated from her hull during the three weeks she has been on station. For two weeks she has not even broken the surface with a periscope. She has remained deep, in the best sound channel. What she faces she does not know.

About 100 miles farther south is the patrol station of the newest Trident submarine, the *Southern State*. Intelligence has been received that an unfriendly foreign power is determined to seek her out and sink her. The cause for this extraordinary decision is not clear, though more than one plausible hypothesis could be suggested: a test of American or NATO resolve, the opening gun of an undeclared war, destabilization of a precarious world peace for the advantage of third parties. There could be others as well. Reaction by the U.S. Navy was prompt. The *Southern State* was directed to shift her patrol station to guard against the possibility that her old one was known. The ambassadors of the countries concerned were summoned to the State Department by an irate secretary. A special meeting of the Security Council of the United Nations was called. Other things, too, were done; most concretely, the *Midwest City* was sent to the vicinity of the Trident sub to render protection.

How to do it? The briefing officer was specific about that. "We don't know where this thing is going," he said. "Maybe there's nothing to it. But we can't take a chance and find out the report should have been believed. Your job is to make sure nobody gets to the *Southern State* from the north. There'll be somebody else guarding her from the south, too, just in case. But if anyone's been sent to make trouble, we think he'll come from the north. It's up to you to hit him before he hits the *Southern State*. Then, when he doesn't report in, they'll think all this over one more time, and maybe that will be the end of it."

"Why don't we just pull the boomer off the line?" the skipper finally dared to ask. His briefer, three ranks and many years senior to him, looked at him unwaveringly for a long moment. "That's exactly what it's about, skipper," he finally said. "You need a picture?"

Submarine lore holds that the best weapon with which to attack an enemy submarine is another submarine. The submarine is a weapon of stealth. Only it can go as quietly, and as deep, and do with such deadly precision what must be done. Only submerged combat can remain unnoticed by the world. The *Midwest City* had been under way for two days when her crew became aware, through a certain preoccupation and various unusual orders their captain began to give, that this was not to be an ordinary cruise.

The ballistic missile submarine, the SSBN or "boomer" in slang, is much bigger than the SSN attack sub. The Trident SSBNs, in particular, are huge by any standard. As big as many battleships of the World War I era, their primary mission is deterrence. Once an SSBN has expended her intercontinental missiles, her operational commanders can either order her back to base for reload or release her to any other operation, such as ASW or antishipping missions, although her huge size can make her less effective. Attack subs, designated SSNs, have several missions, the primary being ASW. Internally, the SSNs are much more densely packed, both with people and with machinery, than the SSBNs. They carry no ballistic missiles, only torpedoes and antishipping cruise missiles. Their operations are much more versatile than those of the SSBNs, and they are also faster and much more maneuverable. The *Midwest City* is one of these subs.

Preceding: The nuclear-powered attack submarine William H. Bates *under way. The ship carries a crew of a dozen officers and ninety enlisted men. Her endurance at sea is limited only by provisions. Mr. Bates, a congressman from Massachusetts from 1950 to 1969, was a popular and influential member of the Armed Services Committee. Naming the* William H. Bates *terminated the practice of reusing the fish names of wartime fleet submarines.*

Facing: As the ballistic missile submarine Nathanael Greene *heads for the Atlantic Missile Range, some of her sixteen Poseidon missile tube hatches are faintly visible on her main deck aft. The* Greene *has alternating crews. Her deterrent patrols average more than two months and are followed by a month's turnaround.*

As she sped to the north, her skipper took careful stock of his situation. Not only must his ship keep from being detected by any possible enemy, it must also remain unnoticed by the submarine it has been sent to shield. He has only a general idea of where the *Southern State* is, but he must maneuver to intercept any attempt to close her position. The closer he can station himself to the *Southern State*, the better sonar guard he can place around her, but at the same time his own sub will be in greater danger; for the *Southern State* has doubtless herself gone to the super-silent condition and will instantly shoot at any submarine she detects. His solution to this was to place himself 100 miles north of the best estimate of where she might actually be. And now he has been there for three weeks of utter solitude, slowly circling, sonar at maximum alert, not daring to do anything that might make noise.

At last, however, there is action. Two whispered words from the control room messenger galvanize everyone in the ship in seconds. "Sonar contact!" Captain and executive officer dash to the sonar room, eagerly snatch the proffered pairs of extra earphones. The displays show new lines in the sea spectrum, but for long moments they hear nothing. Then their ears adjust to the distant frequency, and gradually they begin to hear it. Something is out there, and it is coming nearer. The sound is growing louder. But it is still a long way away, probably at least two convergence zones, perhaps three. For the time being there is nothing to do but wait, and listen, and derive all the information one can from the meager indication. An hour passes, then a second hour. All the sensors of the *Midwest City*'s sonar sets are painstakingly retuned, their responses peaked. So also are her fire control and sonar computers, and her weapons. Nervously, carefully, thoroughly, crew members go through the procedures they have rehearsed so often. The skipper, conducting one of his routine checks through the submarine, senses the confidence all hands have in him and in their ship. But being human, he also worries. Somehow he might fail them and the superiors who have reposed faith in him. Or perhaps, keyed up as everyone is,

tension will create unforeseen problems. But so far, the crew and their equipment are performing according to the drills they have been carrying out for years. And the sound monitors show that, despite all their preparations to engage the enemy, no sound has been released into the water. His ship and crew are aware that they have been noiseless and professional in everything they have done so far, and the knowledge is comforting.

More time passes. The contact is closer. Its true bearing has not changed very much. It is still distant but getting nearer. What is the range? A single bearing does not tell, and any attempt to use the old echo-range method would give the enemy instant warning of the presence of another submarine. But there are other techniques the skipper can try. One of them is to radically shift the *Midwest City*'s own location. This will change the true bearing of the sound source, now coming in clearly. When its bearing is measured carefully from both positions, an accurate computation of the enemy's range can be made. Two or more such maneuvers will not only fix his range, they will also enable the men of the *Midwest City* to determine his course and speed. Almost by way of reflex, the commanding officer gives the orders. Within the hour he possesses detailed information on the other ship. It is definitely a nuclear-powered submarine, and it is heading for the *Southern State*. After much deliberation, he decides to exceed instructions and orders periscope depth to expose an antenna for an instant and query headquarters: Can this by any mischance be a friendly submarine? The answer, classified as urgent and received after his sub has gone deep again, is negative. It begins with the terse information that a NATO submarine is now missing and presumed to have been sunk. The rebuke is only implied, but it is there, and the skipper knows what he must do. The fire control computer is already active, the necessary information long since fed into it. In the torpedo room one of the long-range Mark 48s has been prepared for launching. After a final check of all its systems, the torpedo is released. A long thin wire filament spins out behind it, connecting the weapon directly to the submarine's computers, which aim it toward an intercept position in the enemy's path. The 48 is a fast torpedo, but the range it must cover is long; a tense wait ensues for the anxious watchers. At last the computer indicates that contact has been made. The homing system of the torpedo takes over control, and soon the computer face shows it merging with the target. Suddenly all communication with the torpedo is cut off.

Sound travels more rapidly in water than in air, but the distance to the enemy submarine is considerable. Whatever happened out there is not displayed until some time after it is all over. Then sonar reproduces the enemy's response to the approaching 48: an affrighted burst of speed, frantic maneuvers, the belated release of an unsuccessful decoy. The dull boom of a distant explosion is heard, followed by the sound of emergency air blowing. Enemy propeller beats are suddenly loud, fast, urgent. There may still be some hope for life if they can drive the stricken boat to the surface. Evidently the engine room was not damaged by the explosion. But a flooded compartment has added weight, so much that even the full power of a nuclear engine cannot handle it; the water blown out by high-pressure air does not compensate for that let in by a large rupture in the hull. Desperately, inevitably, the submarine sinks. Deep down, there is a single awful rumble of high-tensile-strength steel collapsing. The watertight bulkheads between compartments have given way under thousands of tons of pressure. Now the hull of the enemy submarine, filled with water from end to end, sinks swiftly and silently. All the men in it are already dead, their bodies ravaged by incandescent heat, fantastic pressure and flying chunks of sharp-edged steel. Their tomb, destroyed, impotent, still retains some of the vestiges of life. It releases millions of tiny bubbles as the black waters force out the secreted air; its propeller is still turning, more and more slowly, as the desperately ordered power fades and deformed bearings grip and gall the smoothly rotating shaft. Finally, all life and movement crushed, the sub strikes the ocean floor, sending a faint, distinctive noise over the *Midwest*

City's sonar. Some of the American sub's crew are jubilant, for the enemy would have dealt the same fate to them, given the chance, and in fact has already sunk a submarine belonging to their allies. Some piously cross themselves and murmur a blessing. All, without exception, are aware that the men now dead, though professionals in another navy, were in the main no different from themselves.

To the crew of the *Southern State*, already on station when the crisis was made known to them, the only change directly affecting their routine was the increased tension resulting from an awareness of their possible danger. That, and their skipper's immediate orders banning noise-making activities. The jogging track in the mid-level of their ship's missile section, complete with banked turns and a resilient surface, was put off limits. Although it was mounted on rubber pads like all of the ship's machinery, self-monitoring noise detectors had shown that a small amount of sonar disturbance was created from the pounding feet of the dedicated sweat squad. The reason for the ban was plain enough; just the same, to the joggers loss of the track was a real deprivation. Its regular use had been permitted whenever the ship was under way. There were crew members who religiously ran several miles a day, afterward relaxing for long periods in the plentiful hot showers with which the ship was also supplied. In the days of battery-powered submarines, adequate water supplies were always hard to come by. In the boomers, which are more accommodating of their crews, the evaporators are tremendous even by nuclear submarine standards, and there are none of the traditional cautions about excessive use of water. Now, however, showers were taboo. The restrictions even went so far as to prohibit loud talking. Not that any such cautions were necessary. Once word of the crisis reached the ship, her crew members had no trouble identifying its possible meaning to them and instinctively set about, on their own, to eliminate all noise.

The emergency, however, brought one advantage in its train. By design, every SSBN patrol included a drill alert. The operational headquarters in Omaha would issue an alert exercise signal which would throw the ship into a simulated nuclear attack. The drill, called WSRT (weapons system readiness test), was carefully differentiated from the highly classified real alert. Simulated instructions would be given and acted on, with all the results automatically entered on telemetry tape for later evaluation. Ultimately a countdown and a simulated missile firing would take place, again with indexed, taped results. When it was done there would be lengthy postmortems, both immediately and after return to port. In one sense the ordeal was welcome, in that once it was over there was presumed to be little likelihood of a second drill. Now, however, posted on bulletin boards in several places in the ship, was a copy of a message recently received: "THIS IS A WAR WARNING. MAINTAIN MAXIMUM READINESS. THERE WILL BE NO WSRT EXERCISES UNTIL FURTHER NOTICE. REPEAT, THIS IS A WAR WARNING." Every crew has its lighthearted, irreverent members. "Hooray for the bad guys! At least there's no more drills!" one of them exclaimed. But nevertheless he, like a number of others, was soon at his locker exchanging his regulation shoes for a soft-soled pair of slippers.

Other than the pervasive atmosphere of increased alertness, the termination of jogging and exercises in the ship's gym, and the noticeably heightened attention given to maintaining quietness during all evolutions, even during movies (thenceforth shown at reduced volume), the emergency had produced nothing new in the shape of the ship's daily routine. It was, after all, exactly the situation for which they had drilled so often, the one for which the ship and all her infrastructure had been created. Meals, served four times a day to accommodate all the watchstanders, were however commented upon for being a notch above their previous high quality. And the cooks noticed that considerably more was being consumed than was the norm. "It's an indication of their suppressed uneasiness," the supply officer told the skipper when the matter came up. "We always see this." All hands in the crew, officers included, also spent more time in their bunks. Commodious by any

naval standard, fitted with individual lights, ventilation and draw curtains for privacy, far enough apart so that one could sit up or at least prop oneself up comfortably for reading, they had been designed with the expectation that men off watch and not otherwise occupied would find them useful for lounging. Until now, this had not been the case; but the onset of hostilities had made the bunks popular. It was almost as though the increased tension in the air made everyone more tired. Or, perhaps, it was just that there was a degree of fatalism in their makeup that, until now, had escaped expression.

Trident and Poseidon submarines carry two types of weapons: the primary intercontinental ballistic missiles, which are the reason for their existence, and conventional torpedoes, located in a torpedo room beneath the control room, for self-defense. The public inevitably hears more about the missiles, since they are so big and the consequences of their being launched are so devastating; but what concerns the crews of these submarines is the condition of the Mark 48 torpedoes. Especially now. If an attack were about to be launched upon their ship, the only weapon with which they could defend themselves would be the 48, and that only if it could do its business before the enemy submarine had itself had time to fire. The thought was sobering enough to assure that every 48 in a torpedo tube had been checked very carefully and very recently. The torpedoman's mates needed none of the queries and admonitions they received from their shipmates. Their torpedoes had never been more ready.

The *Southern State*'s sonar was almost as good as that of the *Midwest City*, but the combat that saved the lives of the SSBN and her men was nonetheless beyond hearing. The explosion that terminated the confrontation was not, however. The sonar instantly identified and reported it for what it was: a torpedo warhead explosion. And then, for an entire day, the terrible question remained: Who was sunk? Will it be our turn next, or was that the end of the danger? It was not settled until twenty-four hours later, when a message from headquarters relieved the anxiety.

Facing: Nuclear submarines so seldom surface that being on the bridge in pleasant weather is a privilege. Here the surface lookout, left, the OOD, right, and the skipper are enjoying their freedom. A lookout watch is also kept from the control room, through the extended periscope and, of course, by radar.

148–49: *The diving control station. In the foreground is the fairwater (bow) planesman, who controls depth and steering. To his left, the stern planesman handles the angle of rise or dive. The diving officer (standing) supervises both men. In the background the chief of the watch monitors hull openings, fittings and tanks.*

150–51: *Flank speed on the surface submerges the bow of a submarine. The dynamics of surface effect are indicated by the bulge of water ahead of her and the hollow just forward of the sail into which she plunges.*

When first conceived by John Holland and others, including novelist Jules Verne, submarines were expected to spend most of their operational time submerged. The strictures of technology earlier in this century, however, thwarted their optimistic suppositions; submarines were really more like surface ships with the capability of submerging for short periods. This was the case throughout the two world wars; submarines of both sides spent far more time on the surface, day or night, than they did submerged and, except for the last years of the Battle of the Atlantic, did far more damage to the other side while surfaced. Functionally they could be likened to old-time torpedo boats with the additional ability to hide in the sea. In the closing years of World War II, Germany introduced the snorkle as a protection against Allied ASW measures, enabling U-boats to operate their diesels while submerged at periscope depth for both battery recharge and increased speed and range. But diesel engines, because of the noise they made, could not be run in the vicinity of enemy ASW forces; and a submerged submarine operating on her battery power alone was mobile only within a very small radius. Sooner or later the sub would have to take desperate chances to replenish air and recharge her battery. Only the fortunate survived the pitiless pouncers lying in wait.

U.S. submarine losses were heavy also, though not nearly so devastating as Germany's. The submariner who has experienced the terror of being pinned down deep beneath the surface by a group of vengeful escorts has an ineradicable memory. Men who felt the power of depth charges exploding alongside their sub, the successive jolts cracking machinery foundations, shaking the massive hull, driving it deeper and deeper, until its heavy steel skin threatened to cave in as they desperately maneuvered (but oh, so slowly!) to dodge the deadly underwater bombs, were already fully conditioned for the promise of nuclear fuel. Power for submerged operation was the block over which their profession had always stumbled. More than anyone else, they could best appreciate the full potential of the nuclear engine.

Nuclear power gives submarines the same benefits it gives to surface ships—speed, maneuverability, endurance beyond measure—and more. Before nuclear power, submarines were submersible boats that were otherwise much like any other ship, hence the term *submersible* that was sometimes used to refer to them. With the reactor, the true submarine was born. To the submariner, the biggest benefit of the reactor, transcending all others by an order of magnitude, is total independence of the need to surface for running diesels, recharging batteries or replenishing breathing air. Nuclear power has given submarines their own special brand of freedom: from the world's atmosphere.

The nuclear engine is a steam engine; it is the source of heat that is different. When control rods are lifted in a reactor, the fuel in its center heats up, as does the highly pressurized water surrounding it. High-speed pumps drive this water through steam generators or boilers, where it takes the place of fire in conventional boilers. The steam generator thus resembles the double boiler used in cooking, in that water controls the amount and speed of heat transfer. A steam generator is not subject to the catastrophes caused by fire or feedwater getting out of hand. Steam pressure can be allowed to vary as it cannot in ordinary boilers. A nuclear-powered steam plant is therefore inherently more stable and easier to operate than an oil-fired steam plant.

Nuclear power does even more than improve the means of operating an engine. To a submariner, crossing an ocean is nothing, anymore. It is like flying, except there are no windows to see through. Sonar takes the place of sight, and one does not have to be at sea for long before one "sees" through a number of other sensors that substitute for those men are accustomed to. It has been repeatedly said that the blind compensate for their lack of sight by improving their ability to smell, feel, touch and hear, and by refining other innate senses, such as the ability to detect the radiant temperature of another body. So it is with the nuclear submariner who has been submerged for months. His sensory apparatus is the equipment that records such data as the depth and temperature of the water and the contour of the sea bottom. Before long the use of these "senses" becomes second nature, and the submariner learns to be a part of the sea environment surrounding him. It is not true that nuclear and electronic technology reduce the feel for the sea that all true seamen have. Additional sensors have given men of the sea immensely better insight into what is happening about them, so that they fear the sea somewhat less and understand it far more. The true submariner is as at home in the sea as the other intelligent creatures who inhabit it.

The *Nautilus* became operational less than ten years after World War II. Had she been around during the previous decade, she might have single-handedly won the entire seaborne Pacific war. Her officers and crew never tired of showing what she could do. There was no war in which to test her, but in the many exercises in which she participated she was a terror to her opponents. ASW forces could not lay a glove on her. She racked up kill after kill in both oceans. She traversed the seas at high speed, always submerged, beyond the ken of any man save her operational commanders and crew. In 1958 she crowned her career with her solitary transit of the Arctic Ocean, passing directly beneath the geographic North Pole. Other submarines came immediately afterward, traveling to the North Pole and elsewhere, circling the entire world, demonstrating range, endurance, speed and reliability. In every aspect of submarining, they surpassed anything that could have been conceived five years earlier. Though their travels were always submerged, in naval circles their visibility was very clear.

Since the first of the SSBN, or Polaris, submarines went to sea in 1960, there has been a succession of improvements in their basic design. Recently, to accommodate a new and far more versatile missile, the Trident II, a bigger ship was designed. Thus was born the Trident submarine, whose type name, like that of its predecessors, the Polaris and Poseidon SSBNs, was taken from the missile it services. Refer-

ring to these huge vessels as boats, as submariners still do, seems hardly appropriate considering their dimensions and displacement, but habit dies hard. With a displacement of more than 18,000 tons, a length of 560 feet and twenty-four missile tubes, the Tridents are ships of the most powerful class, rated by the navy as major combat commands. However, their crews number only about 150 persons, instead of the 1,000 plus of the nuclear-powered guided-missile cruiser *Long Beach* or the 450 or so of the smaller *Virginia*-class nuclear cruiser. Most notable of all is the special manning provision that has distinguished the SSBN submarines: They have two separate crews, a blue and a gold, which exchange places for successive patrols. But even with its two crews combined, a Trident submarine has only two-thirds the personnel of a new nuclear cruiser.

On patrol, the routine in an SSBN is not like that in an attack boat. The SSNs are multi-mission ships and concentrate on training for combat, generally in a one-on-one confrontation. The Tridents and Poseidons train for their primary mission of strategic deterrence. They drill at simulated missile launching, remaining undetected on station, controlling casualties and properly responding to requirements from the national command. They also maintain tactical proficiency in defending themselves against any possible submarine threat and in carrying out their secondary mission of ASW.

While design of the original Polaris ballistic missile submarines was going forward, the navy also readied plans for the first sizable group of nuclear attack boats, the *Thresher-Permit* class of fourteen units. This was followed by the improved thirty-seven-unit *Sturgeon* class and the new, larger and more powerful *Los Angeles* class, which may total as many as fifty-six ships when all are in service. The *Los Angeles* subs (SSN 688 and later) have nearly the same size and displacement as the first Polaris ballistic-missile-class ships, but they have a bigger reactor and main drive turbine and are therefore by a large margin the fastest submarines the U.S. Navy has ever built. Actual performance figures are classified.

One of the more justified criticisms of our submarine force since World War II has been that it has not provided its increasingly fine ships with weapons of commensurate quality. The fiasco of World War II torpedoes, with their malfunctioning exploders, depth mechanisms and steering controls, has been well documented; not so well appreciated is that these obsolete "fish" were virtually the only submarine weapon for many more years. The weapons emphasis during postwar years was on ballistic missiles for the Polaris-Poseidon ships, but these were not the weapons the multi-mission attack submarines needed, nor even what the SSBNs required for their own defense. Development of the long-delayed Mark 48 long-range torpedo took more than fifteen years, while firing exercises with old World War II torpedoes became increasingly unrealistic and submariners increasingly impatient. Now, however, the Mark 48 torpedo is aboard ships and in full production. The Harpoon, a medium-range cruise missile, has been modified for launch from a submerged submarine. Most promising of all the new weapons is the Tomahawk cruise missile. It can be launched submerged, from a regular torpedo tube, to fly extremely long ranges at low altitude. The missile needs no upkeep, so plans have been made to build submersible vertical launch tubes for the Tomahawk into the *Los Angeles*–class submarine's forward main ballast tank; the missiles will thus take up no interior working or loading space.

A cause for concern among submariners in recent years has been the input of new personnel, which has not kept pace with the manning needs of ships. Faced with many years of continuous sea duty in the attack boats, not spelled by an alternate crew as the crews of the ballistic missile deterrent fleet are, many young men did not reenlist when their initial contracts expired or, if junior officers, resigned their commissions when they had fulfilled their minimum obligations. Ideally, all ships with extensive deployment schedules should be double manned. But despite the numerous advantages that might be cited in its favor, such a solution has the disadvantage of adding to costs. Even so, the situation is now greatly improved, as submariners begin to appreciate the privileges that are theirs. To an increasing degree today, the rewards of modern submarine life—the cheek-by-jowl association with the nuclear heart of their ship, which is one of the wonders of the modern world, the use of top-grade equipment of all kinds, the intimate togetherness between friends and contemporaries of like background, the closeness to the sea in all its manifold shapes—have begun to assert their magical fascination. No one can serve in a nuclear submarine without being totally taken with her tremendous potential. True, life aboard may be psychologically strenuous: the physical distance normally maintained between people is cut in half in a submarine; crowds, like those in elevators, are ever present; only in one's own bunk can there be privacy. Most crew members stand watch eight hours out of every twenty-four; if their off-watch time happens to coincide with normal working hours, they pitch in to help their shipmates with whatever repairs or maintenance may be needed. At sea, submariners often log eighty-hour weeks. They do not begrudge the time spent, even if their usual response to the question "What do you do with your leisure time on those long voyages?" is "What leisure time?" The recompense of all this is a feeling of personal accomplishment, an awareness that not many of the world's people share the hidden life that is routine to a man in a nuclear submarine.

To these private considerations can be added the growing if belated appreciation of their contributions and their worth by countrymen who still for the most part cannot comprehend how a submarine works, let alone the nuclear core that gives it life. A growing number of American citizens are willing to accord sailors of the U.S. Navy—and submariners in particular—the respect that is their due for mastering an unusual and specially demanding profession. This is having an effect on the morale of submarine crews. Knowledge that they are succeeding where few can follow is developing pride, without which no one can feel content in life. Private as well as professional satisfaction is trending upward. Herein lies the true reward of a submarine career.

Full power in a calm sea. Two-thirds of the submarine is visible. Her bow extends halfway to the bottom of the picture. A submerged submarine does not lose the power that a submarine does when it roils the water on the ocean's surface. Therefore, the same horsepower drives a submarine faster when she is deeply submerged than when she is at shallow depth or on the surface.

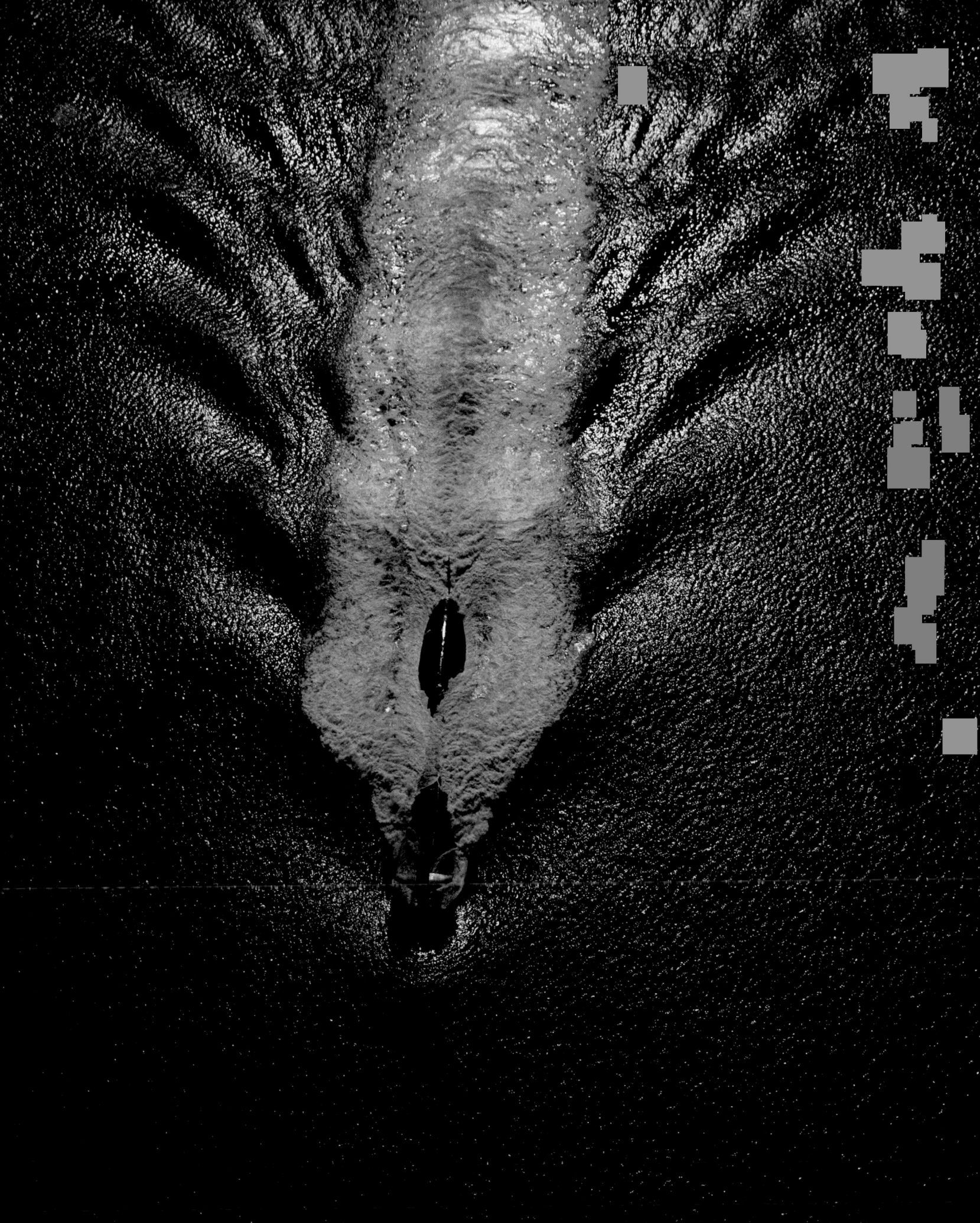

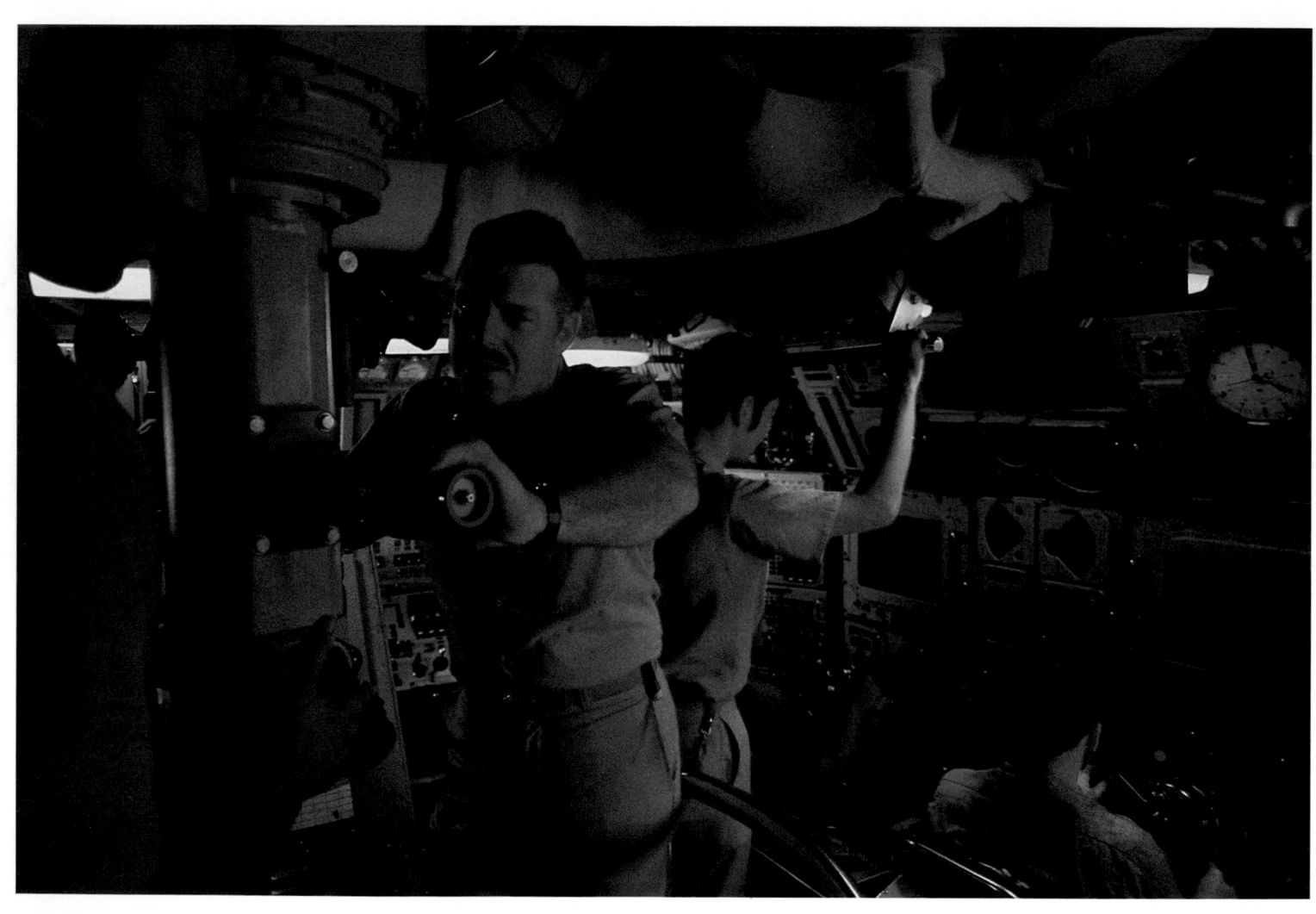

Above: The periscope station, sometimes called the attack center. The captain is about to make an observation. Opposite him stands his assistant, ready to relay instructions and help in other ways. Behind him the diving officer is overseeing the planesmen.

Facing: Technical reference books are everywhere in the navy. This chief and third-class torpedoman's mate have opened the inner door of an empty torpedo tube and placed a testing device in it. Because it is essential that fire control inputs and torpedo sensors function as designed, they must be constantly checked.

Left: In the control room, athwartships from the diving control station, is a small chart desk. Navigating a submarine is like navigating any other ship, except that water depth is a constant concern and there is less working space. The ladder behind the quartermaster leads to the bridge.

Below: The port side of the control room, looking forward. The ship is surfaced, and the maneuvering watch is stationed. In the foreground a sonarman is operating the fathometer. Beyond him the chief petty officer (in khakis) supervises the control room from his post at the ballast control panel.

Facing: The skipper in his stateroom, which is about 8 feet square and contains a folding bunk, a table with seats, a built-in desk, an easy chair, a ship's telephone and communication speaker, and instruments showing course, speed and depth. He sleeps and works here when he is not inspecting or conning his ship. Captains have a lot of paperwork and never enough time.

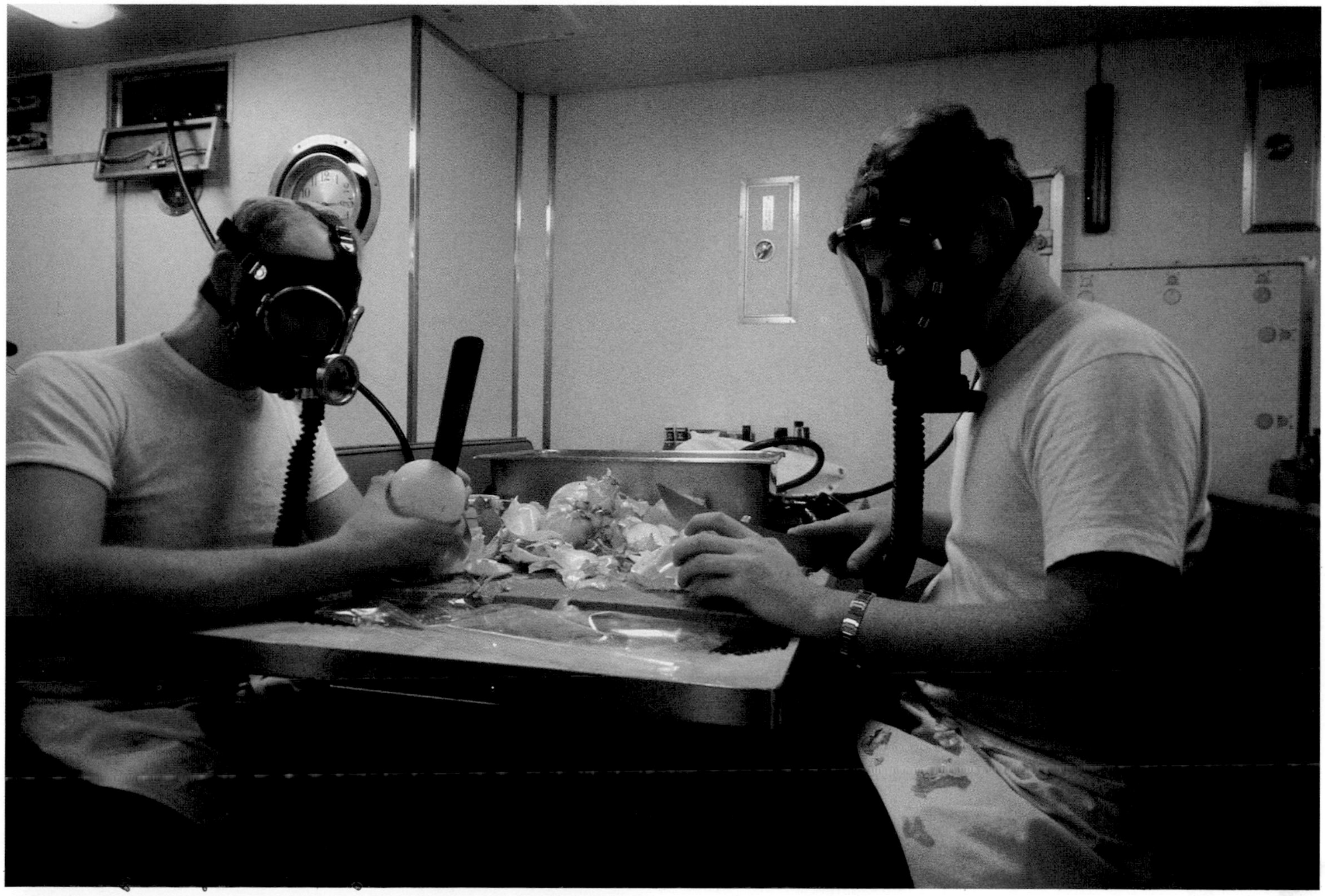

Facing: The galley. Baking is usually done at night, when the cooks are not busy turning out meals for over 100 hungry men.

Above: Detailed as mess-cooks and assigned to slicing onions, these smart men have donned gas masks. The air in a submerged submarine is constantly recirculated.

Consequently, when onions are being prepared, all eyes in the ship water—except, in this case, those nearest the source of irritation.

Left: The mess hall or "crew's dinette." It takes three seatings to accommodate all hands. Under way four meals a day are usually served.

Right: The first Trident ballistic missile submarine, the USS Ohio. *Instead of the sixteen missile tubes of Poseidon and Polaris ships, she has twenty-four; and her Trident missiles are much larger and have longer range than the missiles of earlier subs. For the* Ohio *and her sister ships, the entire world ocean is a potential launching area.*

Below: An Ethan Allen–*class SSN (formerly classified as a Polaris SSBN), with missile tubes deactivated, pulls away from her berth at Bangor. Bangor's function as a Trident missile base began with the arrival of the USS* Ohio, *the first of the huge Trident submarines.*

Right: When ballistic missile submarines are en route to the Atlantic Missile Range for test firings, they have to carry a temporary 100-foot-high mast, specially installed for telemetry and radio. Their speed and submergence depth are limited while the mast is aboard.

Facing: The Nathanael Greene's *Poseidon missile and firing system are undergoing a routine check. Our deterrent missile system is constantly monitored in order to ensure its maintenance at peak performance. Even a test missile can be fired only upon receipt of certain radio signals from higher authority.*

Right: This hand is clutching the firing "key" that launches the missiles. The key is kept in a combination safe, but even when pulled out it cannot shoot a missile until certain operational safeguards have been satisfied. The system is designed so that no one can launch a missile on his own.

These dramatic shots, taken with a high-speed, motor-driven camera, show the launching of a Trident I missile. First the missile, ejected from its tube by steam, pierces the water. For a moment it hangs in mid-air, awaiting ignition of the main motor. Then the missile immediately begins to accelerate into the stratosphere.

Above: The bridge of a submarine leaving port, seen through the open hatch that leads to the sub's interior. Sitting on the bridge turtleback, behind the telephone talker, is the skipper, with binoculars in hand. The OOD is on the left, and the lieutenant on the right holds a walkie-talkie for communication with nearby ships.

Facing: Heading out to the missile range, with a vice admiral aboard. The aiguillettes on his aide's shoulder can be seen at bottom center. The test-monitoring equipment on the bow will be removed when tests have been completed. The ship's readiness will be graded and her officers' careers affected by these exercises.

Seagoing Logistics:
Maintaining the Cutting Edge

A strange convoy proceeds across the sunlit sea, its center a towering forest of masts, stacks and king posts surmounting several gray hulls closely packed together. Surrounding the forest are smaller ships, warships by all appearances, two close astern, several more far ahead, some screening to either side, all steaming steadily. Those on the periphery are patrolling station, weaving, never staying on the same course for long. Their radar antennas are rotating, searching the skies, and their sonars are plumbing the depths.

Closer inspection of the central conglomerate of masts and booms shows that they belong to three ships, proceeding abreast. The largest, dwarfing the other two in size, is in the middle. Thin strands of spidery filaments against the horizon and sky, actually heavy steel wire cables, span the gaps between the replenishment oiler and the destroyers on either side. The cables seem to hold the ships close, so that, seen from any angle except dead ahead or astern, their upperworks appear mingled. The ships are only about 100 feet apart. Between the oiler and each of the smaller ships, and supported by steel saddles curved to prevent kinks, large black hoses hang in great suspension arcs. They are not hanging quietly, however. They are giant anacondas, rebelling at the ignominy of being hung from a wire stretched between two ships. Sometimes they buck and writhe as if alive, as though they had a will of their own, keeping time neither with the gentle and separate rolling cadences of the two ships they connect nor with the lengthening and shortening of the wire spans from which hang their saddles. Impelled by high-speed pumps in the replenishment oiler, fuel is surging through them, and it is this, added to the uneasy motion of the ships, that causes their lifelike restlessness. Through these fuel hoses the replenishment ship delivers the most important part of her precious cargo—and all the while, steadily, in measured pace, the ships move across the azure sea toward the horizon.

As time passes, the ship on the port side of the center group seems to be separating from the other two.

First the hoses are taken from her, retrieved by the behemoth in the middle; then the span wires, which reach from the oddly angled outriggers of the oiler's king posts to the superstructure of the destroyer; and then the highlines, or cargo transfer lines, over which tons of provisions, spare parts and munitions have been passed. Finally, the light telephone and distance lines, marked at 15-foot intervals and extending from deck to deck, are taken in. The smaller ship increases speed slightly, the distance to the larger grows apace—and suddenly, as though the destroyer had been awaiting the moment with pent-up impatience, she goes to full speed. Her wake boils as the magnificent power of her engines flings it astern. She races ahead, her signal searchlight blinking in the direction of one of her fellows in the outer screen. The latter answers, veers sharply, heads in toward the two destroyers in waiting stations astern of the oiler, takes her place last in line.

In the meantime, the ship nearest astern has also increased speed. Swiftly she reaches the just-vacated spot alongside the oiler. Her timing is beautiful; as her bow draws even with the stern of the replenishment ship, she cuts her power. The destroyer's bow dips as her engines answer the order to reduce speed. In a few moments, up it comes with a new surge of engine thrust. She coasts on ahead as her way continues to fall off. Her bridge settles into position alongside the bridge of the replenishment ship, the timing of the power changes having caused her to steady out precisely at formation speed, carefully calibrated while in waiting position astern.

Between the destroyer and the replenishment oiler a deep river races and the sea froths. Larger and heavier waves make up between these running walls of steel. The destroyer's skipper and her OOD are watching the relative motion carefully, to be ready for any sudden sheer out or in, or an unexpected pressure wave slowing or speeding her motion; but she remains locked in place, in equilibrium between the oiler's bow wave and the bank suction effect of the long, deep, clifflike flank of the bigger ship. Aboard the oiler, four men are arming what look like large, single-barreled shotguns. A second man stands beside each, holding a small package from which a thin orange line extends into the muzzle of the shotgun. At an unseen signal four shots are fired; four cylindrical projectiles, trailing orange cord, arc through the air and fall upon the destroyer's decks.

Eager hands aboard the destroyer snatch the shot lines and deliver them to designated stations. More quick-fingered hands pull the swinging cords swiftly aboard. All have messenger lines attached; a dozen or more men fall upon each messenger and heave rapidly, dragging across either a span wire, for fueling, or a highline wire, for transferring supplies. The wires are attached to padeyes on the destroyer's structure by means of pelican hooks extending from strong two-way swivel joints. Fueling span wires are brought across to the destroyer's forward and after fueling stations, and cargo transfer highlines to nearby cargo receiving stations where dry stores and munitions will be brought aboard. All the wires are very heavy, approximately an inch in diameter, and each is held under tension by a hydraulic ram.

Telephone lines are rigged for talk between the bridges and replenishment stations of the two ships, as is the distance line with its color-coded markers for ready measurement of the space between them. Should personnel transfer be planned, a special manila highline, handled by hand instead of by winch, will also be rigged. Ships can be replenished in bad weather until it is unsafe for men to be topside, and at distances up to 300 feet apart (though about 100 feet is considered ideal). Some destroyers throw their bows clear out of water while tethered alongside. Carriers, of course, are so big that almost no sea state short of a wild storm bothers them during replenishment. Their appetites are so great that they may take as many as four span wires with double hoses and a like number of highlines.

The fuel hoses are allowed to slide down the slanting span wires by force of gravity, ugly black loops hanging grotesquely from their roller-equipped saddles. Carefully operated winches that require the

nicest judgment on the part of the men handling them control the speed of descent. The destroyer's probe receiver is hanging at a prescribed distance below the span wire; the probe on the end of the fuel hose is suspended at exactly the same distance as the receiver, which it hits with just the force required to make solid contact. The receiver locks the probe firmly in place and automatically opens its fuel seal. Moments later, the pumps are started and the life-giving fluid begins to flow into the smaller ship's bunkers.

In the meantime, the cargo transfer highlines have not been idle. According to requisitions previously received, great piles of stores—dry provisions, refrigerated goods, fresh vegetables—have already been laid out on pallets on the replenishment ship. Repair parts, drums of lubricating oil, oxygen and acetylene bottles, ship's stores of every description, have likewise been readied. Unlike fueling, which is a mere matter of running the pumps and watching carefully for leaks once the fuel connections have been made, cargo transfers are evolutions of the highest skill and may go on for hours. Before they begin, inhaul and outhaul wires are rigged and a traveling trolley, with a large hook, is placed on the highline wire. Loaded pallets, hung from the trolley, are pulled one after the other along the highline (or allowed to slide down it) and landed gently on the waiting deck of the ship alongside. Then the inhaul brings the empty trolley back to the replenishment ship for the next load.

Frequently the most critical item received during replenishment is munitions, particularly missiles. These must be transferred in a special container designed to fit over the magazine hatch in such a way that the missile can drop into the loading mechanism. The operating standard is forty transfers per highline station per hour, but large missiles cannot be handled this rapidly. A heavy expenditure of munitions may result in a lengthy replenishment. Normally the time is less than one hour, though nearly everyone can cite instances, mercifully rare, when his ship rearmed all night. From the point of view of the oiler's crew, on the other hand, the replenishment process may often seem unending: the successive arrival of ship after ship of a task force, taking their places in a waiting line that disappears over the horizon, can—and often does—mean more than twenty-four hours of back-breaking work.

If fuel is the blood line of a ship of war and munitions her reason for being, mail is the breath of life for her crew. Replenishment ships are like central stations for moving people and mail among a fleet's units. They are the only ships with which contact is at some time or other virtually certain; therefore they act as mail depots, movie exchanges and personnel transfer way stations for a fleet at sea. It is via the replenishment ships that men constantly come and go, reporting for duty or leaving a ship for further transfer, possibly to an aircraft carrier to catch a flight home. The men are transported in an aluminum chair hanging in midair from a line strung between two ships cruising alongside each other at high speed across the sea. Special precautions, beyond those for ordinary transfers, must accompany the procedure. Tension on the highline, for example, is maintained by hand rather than by mechanical winches, which can easily part a line if wrongly adjusted.

The men of logistic ships like to point out that for them, replenishment stations are the equivalent of battle stations, except that a call to replenishment stations is never for drill. Handling huge steel masts and booms with constantly swinging wires from a rolling, pitching platform in a seaway is far more dangerous than pushing the buttons on a fire control computer. No one can sway a heavy pallet of ammunition from one ship to another without wondering when the rig was last inspected. If something should carry away, there will be little time—a fraction of a second—to jump out of the way. Several tons of mast, boom and pallet, sweeping through a wild arc on a broken wire, are lethal to everything in their path. Men go to battle stations on the bridge as well, for in no fleet maneuver is the steering ability of the helmsman, indeed, the exercise of pure sea-

manship by all hands, so demanding. No evolution is so fraught with potential danger as the high-speed maneuvering of huge ships in close quarters, where knowledge of one's ship, of the action of the wind and the sea, and of the laws of physics is crucial. At replenishment stations, some individuals seem to have an intuitive awareness of what is happening around them. Such men never seem to lose sight of the ponderously certain outcome of the events they have set in motion. They have eyes in the backs of their heads, a feel for the sea in the tips of their fingers, and the born confidence of a professional juggler or racing car driver. It shows in the way they handle their heavy gear and in the way they drive their ships.

The operating organization of our navy consists of two home fleets, based, respectively, on the Atlantic Coast (Second Fleet) and on the Pacific Coast and in Hawaii (Third Fleet). These are fundamentally training and staging centers for the deployed fleets: the Sixth Fleet in the Mediterranean and the Seventh Fleet in the far western Pacific (which also includes the Indian Ocean). In Korea and Vietnam and the Persian Gulf, the experience of the Seventh Fleet, its supplies staged through Pearl Harbor, Yokosuka and Subic Bay, is a perfect illustration of the far-reaching problems of fleet logistics.

Resupply of the Indian Ocean battle group was, in the words of the commander of the Seventh Fleet, his principal concern during the Iranian crisis and its aftermath. He had a number of bases to work from, but only the continental United States (with a few exceptions) could provide the huge variety of supplies his ships needed. Everything had to be staged halfway around the world and finally through tiny Diego Garcia or, for the highest of priorities, flown over Africa or from the Mediterranean Sea. Seldom were delivery distances less than 2,500 miles, and roughly 90 percent of all supplies had to come through the tortuously long sea route around Africa or across the Pacific and Indian oceans. Fuel was obtained wherever a contract could be let, but only certain fuels were acceptable, for the navy now operates on highly distilled oil, akin to diesel fuel and not far removed from aircraft jet fuel. For a time a floating fuel farm, a group of chartered tankers, was kept nearby, as were numbers of ammunition ships. Driven by necessity, the commander of the Seventh Fleet became his own traveling ambassador, negotiating for overflight rights here, for docking and shipping support there, authorizing the cannibalization of airplane parts and the exchange of spares within his forces regardless of the immediate state of requisition and paperwork. He and his staff traversed the formidable distances continuously, tackling problems that were, and still are, staggering.

The fast combat support ships, the AOEs, of which there are four in commission, are helping battle group commanders cope with such difficulties. The huge engineering plant for the battleship *Kentucky*— a sister of the *New Jersey*, cancelled at the end of World War II when nearly 60 percent complete—was reclaimed, split in half and installed in the first two AOEs. These are the largest auxiliary ships ever built for any navy. Bigger than anything in our navy except a carrier or a battleship of the type *Kentucky* would have been, they are also very fast. They are rated at 26 knots, although unofficially it is said they can go faster if circumstances require. Early on, battle group commanders formed the habit of keeping them in company, under the battle group umbrella, as an immediate source of resupply. Instead of ceasing action temporarily, replenishment can take place right in the middle of operations. An aircraft carrier today may keep an AOE alongside while she receives planes aboard or catapults them off.

Maintenance of the fleet does not involve only the delivery of consumable supplies to ships at sea. Combatant ships must have regular refits and overhauls far more often than noncombatant ships, for any material deficiency, whether it be battle damage, bottom fouling or machinery breakdown, will reduce combat effectiveness. The need for continuous upkeep and repair has produced the "tender," a mobile repair ship. Wherever our fleet has a base, even a small temporary one, there can be found one of the ubiquitous tenders, generally accompanied by an accumulation of one or more mobile dry docks and an assortment of utilitarian small craft.

The Trident SSBN is the only type of ship planned to break the pattern of forward-based maintenance; it will receive support exclusively on U.S. territory. The first combined operational and refit base is already in use at Bangor, Washington; the second is under construction at Kings Bay, Georgia. Capitalizing on their nuclear fuel and missiles with sufficient range to reach potential targets from most of the ocean area of the world, the Trident SSBNs will need no additional support. The age of nuclear power has given ships unlimited cruising range. Just as coal and steam dramatically shortened the ability of ships to remain at sea, so, now, has the atom dramatically lengthened it again. But submarines deploy for relatively short periods and return to base fairly frequently. Other warships generally remain much longer on station, up to nine months in the case of some recent Indian Ocean deployments. Thus, all surface ships, even the extraordinarily long-legged nuclear ones, need a wide variety of consumable supplies for their crews and, in the case of carriers, fuel and munitions for their aircraft. Periodically all form part of the forest of masts and booms that accompany a fleet replenishment. After all, neither ships nor men can survive on nuclear fuel alone.

The intangible benefits of replenishment are no less important than the fuel, the munitions and the supplies. Ships at sea are little communities adrift in a wild of nothingness, far from home, friends, incentive, inspiration. The action of replenishment, of being alongside another ship, brings a renewal of the spirit. Somehow friendship is all the more cherished by people who meet on the seas after being isolated on its watery stretches. For a few vital moments, two men of the sea can wave to each other, signal with their hands, even yell across the short distance, and thereby refuel one another. They are comrades in a very special sense, in that comraderie of men apart which is a portion of the glue that keeps them whole.

Facing: Personnel as well as inanimate objects can be transferred at sea. But there is a difference: when a man is on the highline it must be tended by other men, not by a machine. A shipmate's hand on a manila line is far more responsive than the oily grip of a winch on a wire cable.

178–79: *Personnel transfer at sea between the USS* Turner *and the USS* Farragut. *The "breeches buoy," originally a lifebuoy with a canvas seat, is now an aluminum chair with flotation gear. Despite stories about unpopular officers being dunked midway, the transfer is more dramatic than dangerous.*

Facing: Underway replenishment may go on for hours. It is a time of furious activity for many crewmen, but others on watch find it boring. A semaphore chat with a buddy alongside helps.

Left: Fueling has been completed and the hoses retrieved, but many loaded cargo nets and pallets must still be transferred on the slanting highline to the ship alongside. Missile pallets must be exactly positioned over the appropriate magazine hatch for striking below.

Above: The Savannah *is a replenishment oiler, a traveling supermarket. She carries fuel, munitions, and dry and refrigerated stores.*

Above: Mobile floating dry docks were what made our forward bases so effective during World War II. They could be towed anywhere. Some were even self-propelled. The USS Edward McDonnell, *a frigate, is ready to be refloated. Her huge sonar dome determines* the shape of her bow and the location of her anchor.

Facing: A ship should be dry-docked at least once a year for optimum performance. The McDonnell *has a single powerful bronze screw. Her turbine can propel her at speeds faster than the 27 knots for which she was designed.*

Facing: Launchings are like the birth of a child, except that more than two parents are involved. There are builders; officials of the state or city for which the ship is named; family and associates if she is named for a person; often former crew members of an older ship of the same name; and the sponsor. This guided-missile frigate, the Stephen W. Groves, *is taking the water at Bath Iron Works in Maine.*

Above: The City of Corpus Christi, *down the ways at Electric Boat Division, Groton, Connecticut. Religious dissension arose when it was announced that this submarine would be named simply* Corpus Christi, *after the city in Texas. The nose of an unfinished Trident sub peeps from the building house on the left, and the nearly completed* USS Florida *broods over the scene from her launching dock.*

Above: The repair ship Vulcan *was the first U.S. Navy operating ship to be manned partially by women. The* Vulcan, *a noncombatant, spends more time working on other ships in port than under way herself. Ensign Carlton is OOD in port, on the enclosed quarterdeck, and may well qualify as OOD under way.*

Facing: Pamela Bilstab is a second-class boatswain's mate and on the way up. The USS Vulcan *was authorized 66 women among her crew of 730 for a 1979 Mediterranean deployment, the first time female sailors went abroad as members of a ship's company.*

188–89: *Inside the Trident repair facility at Bangor, Washington. SSBNs fitted with the new long-range Trident missiles are on patrol station as soon as they leave a U.S. port. They need no forward basing to get them quickly into action; hence, their repair facilities are concentrated at home base.*

Theory and Practice:

Developing
the Skills

Sailors learned to operate the large machinery of the Industrial Revolution on the job. Machinists received their training as apprentices, servicing the mammoth mechanisms that drove their ships with rag and oilcan in hand. Firemen learned their trade in front of the shriveling heat of white-hot fires. Then technology forged ahead, and the horizons opened. Steam engines produced electricity. The wonders of electricity led to radio, then radar, electronics and, finally, microelectronics. Today watching a computer run is no more sufficient for learning how it works and how its needs are serviced than reading a law book is sufficient for passing the bar examination. Since the advent of electronics, the navy has had not only to keep abreast of technological advance but to remain in its vanguard. In the face of ever-proliferating computers, *ad hoc* training programs, no matter how well planned, can no longer do the job. Apprenticeship is a thing of the past.

After enlisting in the naval service for the first time, today's recruit reports to Orlando, Florida, Great Lakes, Illinois, or San Diego, California, for eight weeks of basic training. During this period he will be taught some of the fundamental skills of the seaman and will be exercised at close-order drill to drive home the value of teamwork. Boot camp's first task, however, is to introduce the recruits to an entirely new way of life. The haircut, the first laying on of hands by the military organization, is a symbolic watershed, a visible act separating them from their previous existences. At the end of eight weeks of indoctrination in naval customs and traditions, they are no longer the motley crew that stumbled over the threshold onto a new career, and they are proud of it. A graduation ceremony marking the end of basic training is preceded by a formal parade before reviewing officers, families and friends, and, far from unimportant, before newly arrived recruits starting their own careers. Then the graduates gleefully leave boot camp forever, most of them unaware how profoundly their lives, bearing and outlook have been affected by the experience just behind them, or how much detailed training lies ahead.

Preceding: Graduation day parade after completion of eight weeks of boot camp at Orlando, Florida. Recruit training has been described as severe culture shock. At its end, these young men have their feet firmly planted on the ladder to advanced rate and responsibility.

Recruits are also subjected to the first of a barrage of aptitude tests and preference questionnaires that will continue throughout their enlistments. Upon graduation, about one third of them will receive orders to additional training in another section of the boot camp compound—with higher status, more liberty and far more freedom than the crop of new recruits replacing them. There they receive a month's basic training as airmen, firemen or seamen, depending on ability and preference; after that they report to their first ships, if possible in the areas of their own choice. The remaining two-thirds of the graduates have screened for orders to "class A school" to spend several months learning special skills. Until the rate to which they aspire, say radioman, is made, they are known as strikers for that rate (in this case, radioman strikers). In due course, they take examinations and, if they pass, are promoted to the rank of third-class petty officer, the lowest rung in the ladder of their particular rate. Specially qualified individuals, after finishing class A school, go on to class C school for still higher training. Some men may progress through a succession of schools learning technical skills and spend more than a year under instruction before reporting to their first ships. Ultimately, however, most will go to sea, for there, by definition, is the navy.

Officer procurement is similar to enlisted recruiting in many respects, except that it involves more stringent entrance examinations and more difficult qualification criteria. The most highly prized avenue to commissioning is the Naval Academy at Annapolis. There, after four years of strenuous academic studies, those who survive the curriculum—the attrition rate can be as high as 25 percent—become ensigns in the navy or second lieutenants in the marine corps. The Naval Reserve Officer Training Corps at universities authorized to have such units is another way of obtaining a commission; a third is the Officer Candidate School at Newport, Rhode Island, which candidates attend after graduation from college.

Training no longer terminates upon graduating from boot camp or receiving one's commission, however.

Notices of all kinds constantly solicit applicants for one or another of the great number of navy schools or for special navy programs and courses offered at factories or in universities. One of the most competitive programs is flight training school, based primarily at Pensacola, Florida. For both officers and men this leads to complete reorientation of life and career. Surface ship officers go to the fairly recently inaugurated surface warfare officer's school, which probably has the largest attendance of all navy officer schools. For those interested in the undersea there is the submarine school at Groton, Connecticut. Graduates of both surface warfare and submarine schools undergo selection for nuclear power training. Only some surface officers, but virtually all submariners, receive this additional training. And once a year a new class of officers, those most academically oriented, attend certain institutions for technical studies leading to the designation Engineering Duty Only. Similarly, the supply corps school, located at Athens, Georgia, graduates officers bearing permanent supply corps designators.

The navy's unprecedented need for intensive training was answered by the creation in the early 1970s of the post of CNET (chief of naval education and training). Not only must the CNET see to it that all ships and stations have men qualified to use the navy's evermore complex equipment, he must keep account of that new equipment in the design stage, ensure educational support for its operation and maintenance, and issue full information to all commands on the programs created to train people to use it. He deals with a whole new form of accounting merely to keep track of the proliferating courses and graduates. Any person who receives formal training of any length has a designator (if he is an officer) or an NEC (naval enlisted classification) symbol entered on his service record. Changes or additions to an individual's codes and designators, and to the requirements of his billet, are made constantly. Each ship has its own specifications for the necessary technical expertise required in each of its billets; among all the ships of the navy the abilities of 600,000 plus officers and men must be spread as equally as possible. Bringing order to this chaos is a large computer complex in Washington, D.C., where names, ratings, ranks, NECs and qualification designators are kept current for everyone on active duty.

It is in the most advanced training that the full impact of new electronic technology is felt. Computer simulation has paved the way for the use of mimic environments in training procedures. The missile-firing SSBN submarine fleet, in which each ship has two rotating crews, has taken advantage of such sophisticated electronic techniques. To keep a crew at the peak of effectiveness between patrols requires a degree of realism in training facilities never before achieved. At Bangor, Washington, in the new Trident submarine base, an individual can lose himself entirely in his mock surroundings and emerge, hours later, feeling as though he has actually stood a watch at sea. Inevitably, however, his watch was studded with emergencies deliberately planned to be far more strenuous than any ordinary circumstances. And at naval flight school in Pensacola and elsewhere, such simulation, its accuracy honed to the finest details of operations, is used to train and maintain the skills of pilots. Instructor- and computer-programmed inputs are fed into the instruments of dummy gymbal-mounted cockpits. Computer-generated scenarios are similarly employed in the training schools for radar and sonar operators, missile technicians, those manning the new gas-turbine main propulsion systems—in fact, in any school where simulation is crucial to producing highly qualified individuals.

To its credit, the navy foresaw that the wholesale education of naval officers and crewmen had to usurp the position of apprentice training on board ship in order to keep up with the electronic revolution. The necessary adjustments were made, and not a moment too soon. Thus the past decade has seen the creation of what might be termed the professional specialization echelon of the navy's broad-based training program. Thanks to this, the old saw about navies preparing only for the past war is no longer true.

Left: After completion of their first year at the Naval Academy at Annapolis, former plebes carry out an Academy tradition: the person who can replace the hat glued on the peak of the greased Herndon Monument with his own will be the first admiral of the class.

Bottom, left: A classroom at Officer Candidate School, Newport, Rhode Island. The master chief boatswain's mate, wearing six hash marks denoting twenty-four years' service and a chestful of ribbons that include the Silver Star for gallantry in combat, is demonstrating the use of booms and wires to hoist in a vehicle.

Bottom, right: NROTC midshipmen wear their uniforms only on specified drill days and are not otherwise distinguishable from their peers. In return for room, board, tuition and navy pay while in school, they attend weekly indoctrination drills and serve from three to five years after college.

Above, left: Graduation week at Annapolis witnesses old traditions alongside new activities. For those who double as parents and alumni, it is a time for renewing old friendships and taking stock of how the Academy may have changed. The navy's Blue Angels highlight the festivities.

Above, right: Another event is a regatta staged by the Academy sailing squadron and featuring a formal review of the midshipman yawl fleet.

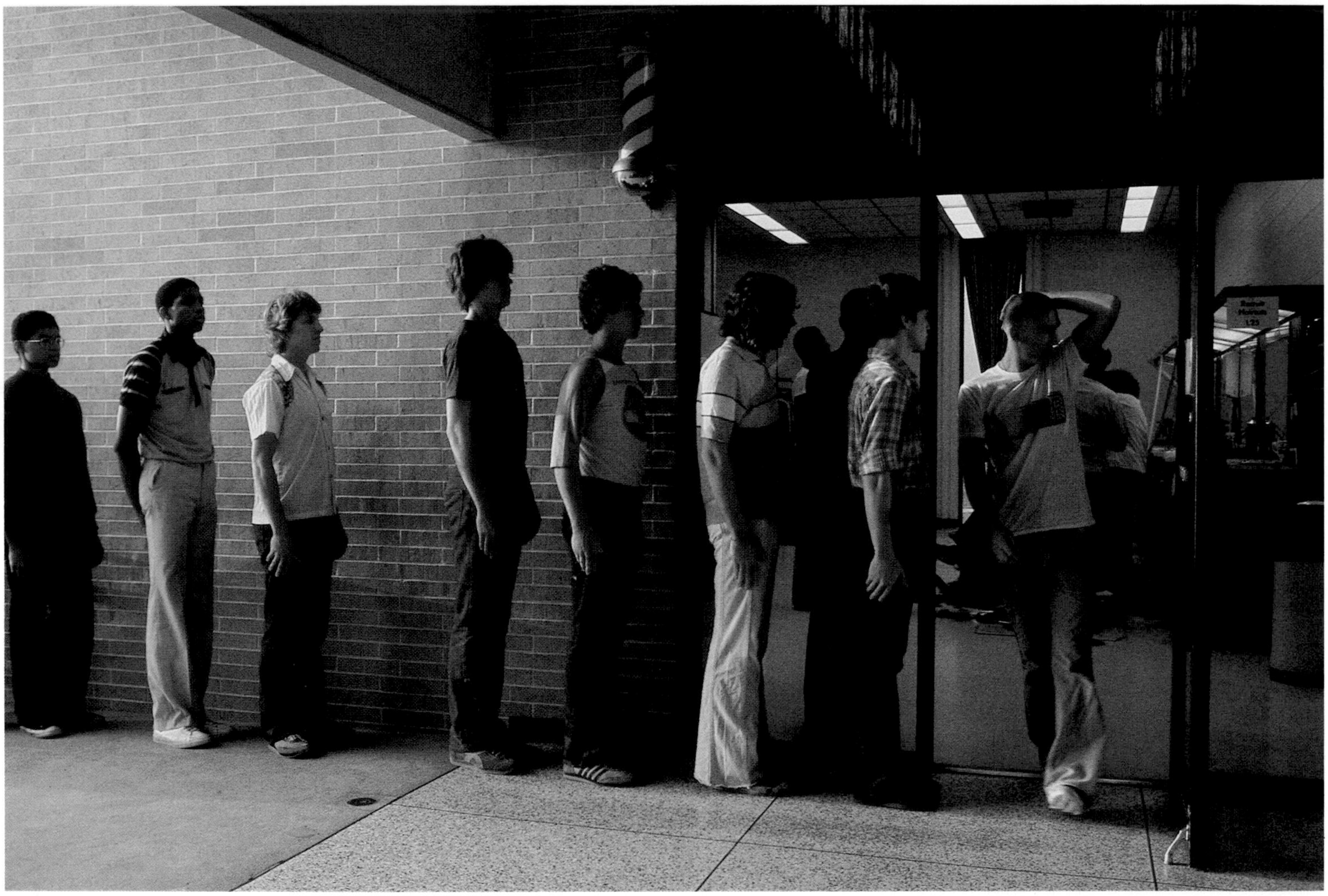

Left, top: Whether it is boot camp or the Naval Academy, the first order of business is the military haircut, which leaves little showing but the skin covering the skull. The barbers are easier on females, but most women report with their hair already cut to regulation.

Left, bottom: The young man in the chair seems resigned to a real "butch." In earlier days there was a need to extract tics and fleas from a farmboy's hair, but nowadays the close cut is just a routine part of the stressful change from civilian to military life.

Above: The first formation. Already quite a bit of indoctrination has taken place. In the next step uniforms will be issued, completing the dramatic transition to a new kind of life. Training will quickly progress beyond the traditional seamen's arts, for the navy today is technically oriented.

Below: Damage control is one of the most important functions of a navy crew. All recruits receive fire-fighting training in their first weeks and periodic refreshers thereafter.

Bottom: Poison gas training. The gas used here, although smelly and uncomfortable, is not in fact hazardous.

Facing: The recruit, dressed in fire-resistant clothing, is entering a burning compartment. The instructor, holding a spray nozzle, will keep a protective veil of fog in front of the trainee while he carries out his mission.

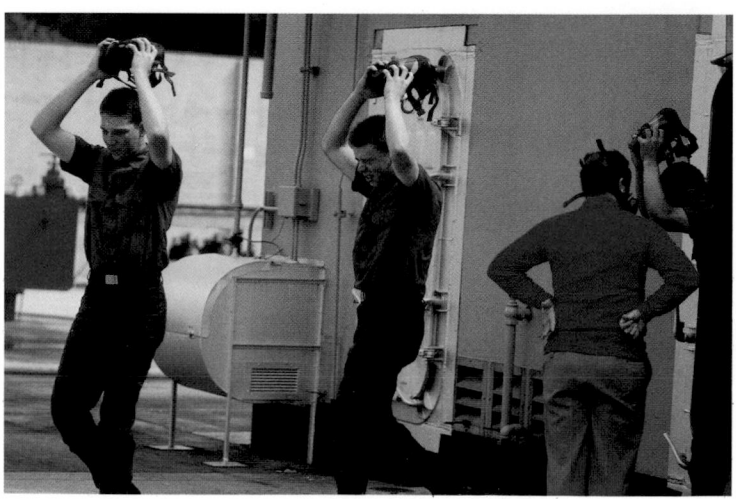

Facing: A graduating officer candidate at Newport is fitted for her officer's cap at the naval uniform shop. The feel of that first cap must be experienced to be understood. It stands for the sweat the candidate expended in the earning of it, and the trust and confidence thereby reposed in her abilities and integrity.

Above: The euphoria of the day is vibrant in the air. Graduation has taken place; boot camp is over forever. On to the bus for the next duty station: perhaps a ship, perhaps a school for more training. The inner man is the same, but his outer transformation is complete. He's in the navy now!

Above: BUDS (basic UDT/SEAL) training is the toughest in the navy. After rigorous conditioning, recruits must endure six harrowing days of "hell week" without sleep or even rest. One of the many demanding tasks to be performed is crossing the "Black Lagoon" on a vibrating rope over smoke, dust and explosives.

Right: BUDS training lasts six months and is, of course, all volunteer. Climbing repeatedly over a tall cargo net against time, running 10 miles at sunrise, marching all night, trekking long distances through deep mud, parachuting from low-flying aircraft and scuba diving under darkness—all are routine exercises.

Facing: In the submarine base at Bangor, Washington, realistic emergencies can be created. A fixture has burst under pressure at deep depth. Locating and sealing the breaks with emergency clamps can mean life or death to the crew of a submerged submarine.

Below: The diving-control-station mockup is used for training. Dials give appropriate readings, and controls look, feel and operate like the actual ones in Trident subs. The entire compartment tilts down or up according to the degree of dive or rise, or to the side in a simulated high-speed turn.

Left: In the same building is a complete Trident-missile-tube installation, extending the full height of the structure. Close under the roof girders is a mockup of the sub's main deck with a missile tube hatch. A plastic membrane is being lowered over the missile's nose cone.

Above: There are ways of getting things done in the navy that would never be accepted in civilian life. Before the sailor goes through the pay line he must go through the ship's inoculation checkoff line, where immediate action can be taken to ensure that he has all the required shots.

Top, right: Hospital ships, protected by the international Red Cross symbol, were until recently the only ships that had females—doctors and nurses—aboard. The repair ship Vulcan was the first navy ship not so designated to have women as part of her regular crew.

Bottom, right: Dental as well as medical care is one of the benefits of naval service. Aboard the Vulcan the dental technician may be female. If the ship comes under attack, she goes to a battle station just as the male crewmen do.

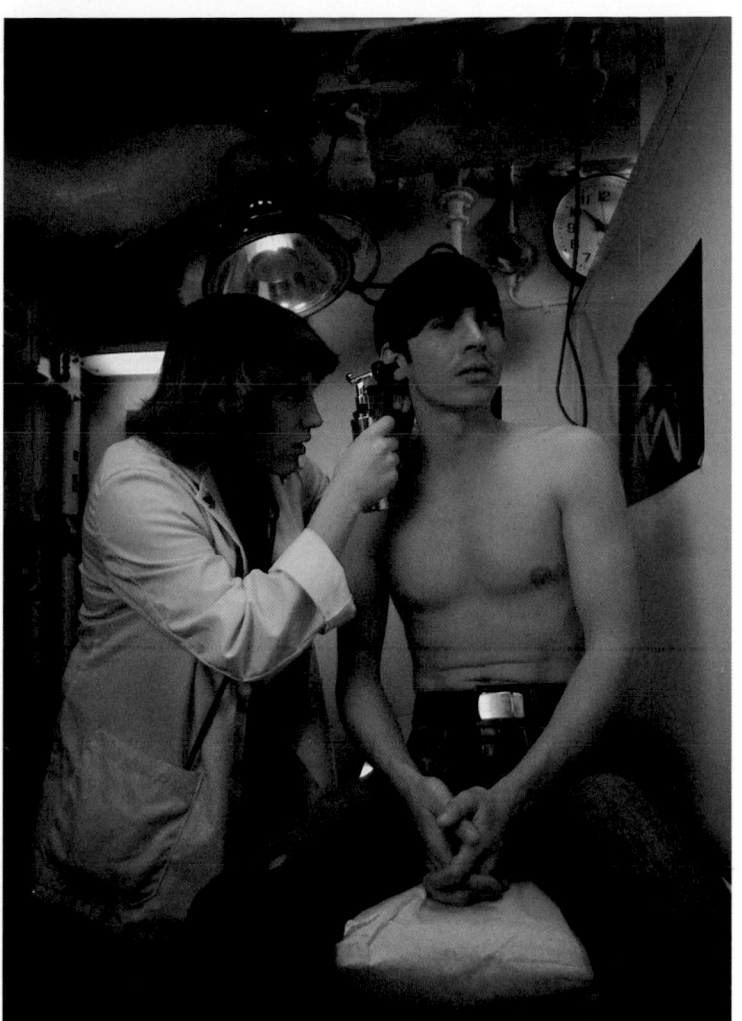

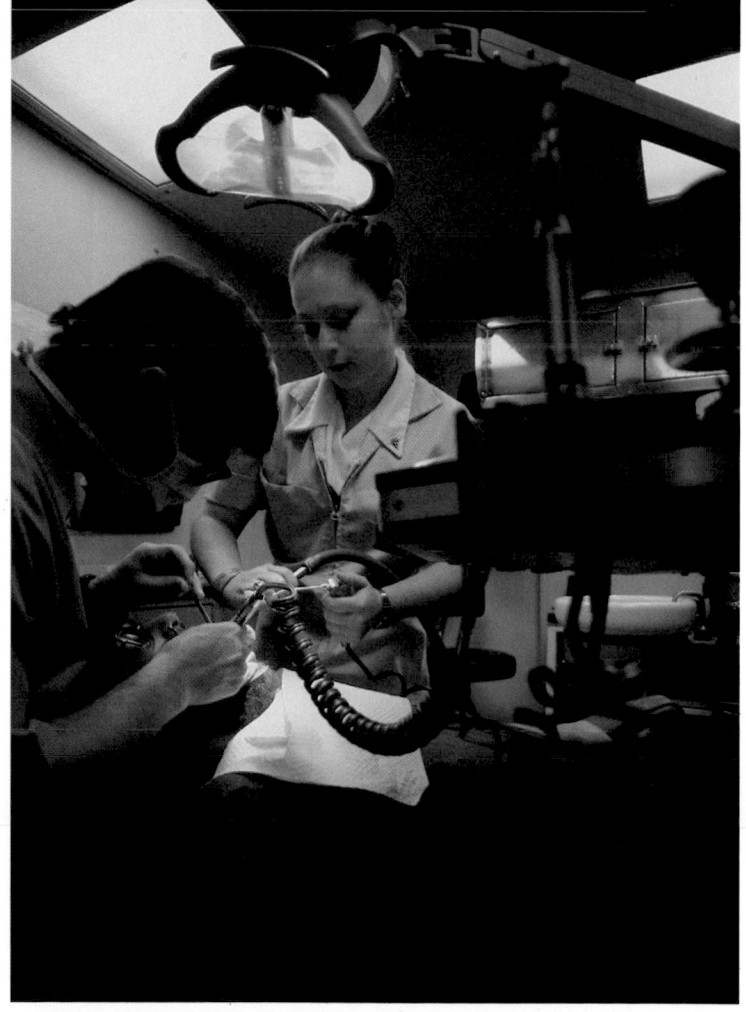

Above: In a decompression chamber at the submarine base escape-training tank, Pearl Harbor. Seventy-five people were treated here in 1979, the majority of them civilian divers needing emergency help for the "bends." All submariners must qualify in escape procedure.

Right: Maggie O'Rourke's shoes weigh 35 pounds, her helmet 54 and her belt 84. With other odds and ends her outfit comes to a total of 186 pounds. It is in the height of fashion where she plans to wear it. Maggie's navy rating is EM3 DV (electrician's mate third class, qualified diver).

Putting it Together:

From Sea
to Land

t was a marine sergeant in World War I who was credited with the shout "Come on, men! Do you want to live forever?" The country is accustomed to the cry "Send in the marines!" when conditions seem to be getting out of hand. There is no question that the image of the U.S. marine is that of a first-class fighting man. This is what he has been trained to be. He has also been trained to follow orders rigorously, exactly, and without question. The result conjures up another image, an unfair one: that of the automaton who applies neither thought nor interpretation to the instructions he has received. These two views must be separated; for though the marine at his police or sentry post can and should be rigid in carrying out his duties, the marine corps everywhere emphasizes the necessity of maximum flexibility in performance of its primary function, projecting national power from the sea to the land. One has only to participate with marines in the preparation of an amphibious operation, large- or small-scale, to recognize the breadth of expertise and creativity professional marine officers can bring to the planning table.

Responsive planning and execution are basic to amphibious doctrine, even though certain principal operational constraints cannot be disregarded. An amphibious battle group is never small. The contingencies it may have to face are too many, even in the best of circumstances, to be handled by a small number of ships. There are in fact likely to be three distinct battle groups associated with any landing: a carrier battle group providing air cover, a surface battle group prepared for shore bombardment if necessary, and the amphibious group itself. The first priority is to establish sea and air control throughout the amphibious objective area, overwhelming the enemy's air potential, cutting him off from logistic support, and leaving the beleaguered garrison to its own devices.

Ideally, the power having been established, at this point it should not need to be used further. History has shown, however, that mere demonstration of the ability to force capitulation is seldom sufficient to produce it. A test of wills is anticipated in all operations plans. Imagine now that a full assault landing against desperate opposition is required. In the darkness before dawn, from over the horizon, deep-lying grey hulls approach the until-then-undisclosed point of assault, and shore bombardment begins with first light. Fused for minimum penetration of the earth, loaded with high explosive for maximum surface blast effect, the shells of an efficient bombardment make a shambles of earthworks or hand-built fortifications. Few defenses can stand against a direct hit by a 16-inch projectile, and smaller shells have a proportionally devastating effect. The roads, the landing fields, the infrastructure of the place, all the communications facilities, all the buildings, even the forests and the surfaces of hills, are smashed into bits, demolished. If the bombardment goes on long enough there may be little more left than pulverized mud and sand and shattered trees, as though a giant Rototiller had crisscrossed the land again and again. Then another fleet of grey ships moves in close: amphibious assault ships, transports, tank landing ships (the ubiquitous LSTs)—a veritable armada, organized and in fact built for the single purpose of projecting power ashore. Most of the ships have helicopter flight pads; some, the amphibious assault ships (LHAs), except for subtle differences, resemble aircraft carriers, which in a sense they are, being equipped for V/STOL (vertical or short takeoff and land) aircraft. As the armada approaches, groups of helos rise off the decks of all the ships that can handle them. Within minutes the air is full of helicopters flying briskly inland. Meanwhile, flights of combat-capable V/STOL Harriers lift off from the largest of the new arrivals. At the same time, one particular group of ships, distinguished by great, forward-leaning, derricklike structures surmounting their bows, heads straight for the shore. High overhead are the carrier battle group Hawkeyes with their huge radars. These are the eyes of the carrier CICs, which enable the distant commanders to maintain a moment-to-moment picture of what is going on within the areas of their operational responsibility. At a lower level, Harriers and other conventional aircraft, plus helos equipped with dipping sonar,

Preceding: Invasion of the coast of California. This is one of many such practice landings carried out each year by the U.S. Marine Corps.

Facing: The face of a fighting marine. He is wearing a flak jacket and carrying an M16 rifle. This is only an exercise, but that does not rule out the use of live ammunition. Strict discipline is in order.

ceaselessly circle the assault area, flying cover to discourage any nascent effort to attack the assault force by air or any other means. They are particularly watching for close-in submarines, which might have remained secreted until now, and any concealed and still effective fortifications. This is the time of greatest danger to the amphibious assault forces, when they are most vulnerable to any determined resistance. The tank landing ships drive in close to shore, anchor by the bow and stern, and sling an aluminum ramp onto the beach so their tanks can roll off. Farther offshore, the dock landing ships and assault ships have been disgorging great numbers of boats from specially designed wells in their sterns. Once launched, successive waves of assault craft form up and head for the beach. Within a very short time a strong force has landed and begun to set up the first of the beachheads.

While the attention of the defenders is concentrated on the developing beachhead, helicopter-borne troops are being landed behind enemy lines. The troops in the first helo to touch down will instantly deploy to cover the second, those in the second will augment them to cover the third and so on, rapidly widening and consolidating the area chosen for initial landing. Then, with helos, Harriers and more conventional aircraft from the distant carrier battle group providing close cover, perhaps over a convenient airfield, heavy lift helicopters will bring in light tanks and other assault vehicles. As always, speed and exact scheduling (because of the interdependence of so many other sequential functions) are of supreme importance. The vertical envelopment force has been tasked to push immediately toward the beachhead, pinch out, capture or destroy the enemy, and convert all the area covered so far into an enlarged air and beach landing zone. If information about enemy capabilities has been correct, the helicopter troops and the beach assault forces can be linked up within the time allotted. If there are difficulties for which allowance has not been made, there will be delays; and delays will cost lives, sometimes far out of proportion to the degree of the setback itself.

The danger to troops landing against opposition is always very high, the casualty rate tremendous. But this is nothing new to marines, who have always looked danger in the face. Originally they served aboard men-of-war to keep order among the crew, to act as snipers from the fighting tops in battle, and to form the nucleus of landing forces that might be organized from a ship's crew. In the navies of the eighteenth and nineteenth centuries, amphibious operations were invariably organized when the need arose, on the spur of the moment, and were characteristically a jumble of improvisations. Farsighted U.S. marine officers had long demanded better planning for such expeditions, and many built service reputations on their ability to get a proper landing operation going when required. Their prayers were answered when General Lejeune became commandant.

If the marines have a patron saint anywhere near the stature of the navy's Alfred Thayer Mahan, it is John Archer Lejeune, commandant of the marine corps from 1920 to 1929. While in charge of the Marine Barracks at Quantico, Virginia, in 1916, during his service in World War I in France, where he was one of General Pershing's most trusted army division commanders, and until his retirement after his term as commandant, Lejeune studied the British attempt to force the Dardanelles in 1915. The attack, made by sea and by amphibious landing on the Gallipoli Peninsula, had been an unmitigated disaster. Lejeune was appalled at the amateurishness of the operation. Even so, it would have succeeded had its leaders not been inept. Almost immediately after assuming command of the marines, he directed a full-scale study of all aspects of amphibious warfare; virtually all marine officers were ordered to dissect every facet of the Gallipoli debacle. At the time, navy war plans revolved principally around ORANGE, the code name for Japan, and Lejeune correctly predicted the requirement for forcible landings against strong and even fanatical opposition. However, with the British experience in the Dardanelles in mind, he knew that no force then existing, his marines included, was truly amphibious. Attainment of an amphibious capability thus became one of his main objectives as commandant of the corps, and though he did not live to see it realized (he died in 1942), the success of the navy–marine corps team in the Pacific island campaign was in large part due to the program he instigated.

Thanks to Lejeune's vision, plans for amphibious operations today are buttressed by organization, foresight and discussion. Careful operational distinctions now lend clarity to a once little-understood subject. When someone says "amphibious landing," he is referring specifically to marines coming unopposed from the sea to a foreign shore, but without the benefit of harbors, piers or airfields. If he says "amphibious assault," he is speaking of marines landing through enemy fire, vulnerable on the water and at the landing site during those critical initial moments, then consolidating, organizing and moving inland to a more defensible position. Vertical envelopment or vertical assault means an assault landing by helicopters behind enemy lines. The amphibious assault, a U.S. Marine Corps specialty, differs in one extremely significant detail from any other type of military attack or invasion. An army marching across a border starts from its own camps, bringing a logistics train with it. If an army goes overseas in support of an ally, it brings convoys of supplies to the ally's friendly harbors. The amphibious force, in contrast, lands on the beaches with nothing. Troops have to fight their way ashore and have only the weapons and ammunition they can carry with them. Their first and most vital task, after landing, is to make preparations for receiving supplies of all sorts—food, water, shelter, fuel, ammunition. Within not days but hours, everything they need must be where it is expected, ready for instant use. Combat loading ships is an art the marines have necessarily developed to an exact science. Nothing can be left out, forgotten or even out of normal order. The beachmaster—a title born of wartime experience—fulfills a crucial function during the frantic hours of bringing it all ashore to the right place and in the right sequence.

Under the best of circumstances, an amphibious assault is never easy. Critics have even maintained that it cannot succeed against a determined enemy, that assault forces, so terribly exposed at the outset, will always sustain unacceptably heavy losses. Such arguments were also heard both before and after Gallipoli, even though facts showed that failure was due to entirely different causes. The other side holds that such assaults can be successful if proper planning by experienced personnel is completed in advance. Each operation presents a different problem that must be tackled by solutions and techniques peculiar to it alone. So says marine corps doctrine. Some assaults will always be more difficult than others, but what seems impossible to an amateur planner may look very different to a trained and skillful one (as the Germans showed when they defeated France's vaunted Maginot Line).

Marines, trained as combination sea and land soldiers, respond to the appellation "soldier" as a matter of course. In bringing power from sea to land they are tasked with the indispensable transition function: to make the assault landing, create and defend the beachhead, and make all preparations for whatever is next planned. If the assault is on an island like Iwo Jima, the marines will perform the entire operation. If the target is larger, it may be necessary to bring in army troops, as at Inchon, Korea. In such case, after establishing the staging area and setting up debarkation and other temporary port facilities, the marines turn responsibility over to the army. In the combat-ready, air-sea-to-ground marines, the nation has its only dedicated ready agent for a forcible landing against opposition. The "web-footed soldiers" can proceed directly, without hesitation, via air and water, from a sea operation to one on land, holding their beachhead and opening the way for the follow-on army forces that may be needed for a sustained land campaign.

The marine corps' smallest ready force is the MAU (marine amphibious unit). Normally with around 1,400 men, the MAU is too small for employment in any but the simplest circumstances. It can, however, be maintained in instant readiness, aboard ship or ashore, for initial action in the emergencies that con-

218–19: *This gunnery sergeant ("gunny") will get no prizes for making his audience feel at ease, nor is that his intent. The rain and slush have to be accepted, and the gunny's "frag" order (a fragment of the operation order giving their objective and other very basic items) committed to memory.*

220–21: *A clandestine landing during darkness by SEALs, special forces personnel who have received the toughest navy training possible. With no support other than their wits and stamina, they will steal into enemy territory in small groups to carry out unconventional warfare missions.*

Once these preliminary launches are completed, flight operations begin. Some planes, such as the F-14 Tomcats, are sent on combat air patrol missions to provide instant readiness in case anything untoward—such as the sudden approach of unfriendly aircraft or fast patrol boats—should take place. Two planes of the *Nimitz*'s combat air patrol were attacked by Libyan jets in the Mediterranean in 1981, creating the well-publicized incident in which the latter were shot down by the highly professional Tomcats. Other planes, such as A-6 Intruders or A-7 Corsairs loaded with small bombs, might be sent on practice attack or reconnaissance missions. Some are equipped with air-to-surface missiles, practice or real, while others carry practice bombs, or camera or gun pods. All the planes are sent out in groups, the smallest comprising at least two aircraft for mutual support. The missions that a combat plane can fly are of course limited by its design parameters, the types of weapons available to it and a host of other technical factors. Within these constraints, however, its missions are curbed only by the imagination of the pilot and the controllers. A modern aircraft carrier is a most versatile ship of war, able to employ her planes in ways no one could foresee when naval aviation was first conceived.

Upon completion of their missions, returning aircraft form a landing pattern before being recovered on board the carrier, immediately following the last launch of the next succeeding cycle. Landing on a carrier deck that looks like a moving postage stamp puts maximum pressure on a pilot. Jetliners coast long distances after touchdown, but carrier planes land like birds, wings braking against air, legs extended forward to snatch a branch or twig. A carrier pilot aims for a wire stretched across the runway, ideally the third of the standard four, and comes in with a pronounced tail-down attitude, speed brakes on full, engines at 75 percent power, air speed, in some aircraft, as high as 140 knots. The plane is dropping fast, and in order to guide it the pilot must keep a lighted orange ball centered in the landing mirror on the carrier's deck edge. He is "on the ball," in the slang of "tailhook-

ers." If all goes as intended, he will clear the after end of the armored flight deck by 15 feet and slam his plane down on it in a "controlled crash." He hits the deck with 50 to 80 tons of impact, many times that of a commercial airliner on a concrete runway.

When the tailhook of the plane "grabs" one of the four wires reaching across a carrier's stern, the two greasy inch-and-a-half-diameter cables to which the ends of the specially woven and hardened arresting wire are connected are snatched through their fair-leads at lightning speed. The sheaves on each end jerk into furious rotation, and the two great metal housings in each arresting gear engine room crash violently together. They weigh tons. The noise is tremendous, a virtual explosion; fine droplets of oil and grease are flung everywhere, spraying the men standing watch near the monster mechanism. It is their privilege to curse the day they were detailed to the job, but the only thing of consequence is to keep that incoming plane from going beyond the 300 to 400 feet of allowed run and over the forward edge of the landing strip. When an arresting gear engine explodes into life, it alone, with its wire and sheaves, must halt a 30-ton plane tearing down a short runway at up to 140 knots.

The moment the wheels strike the deck is the most critical in the entire flight. The pilot's pulse and blood pressure are at their highest. He throws his throttle forward to full power. If his tailhook has missed or bounced clear of all four wires, he has about three seconds to get the speed brakes retracted before flying again. If his tailhook snags one of the wires, he will instantly feel his harness dig painfully into his shoulders and belly as the 70-ton pull yanks his plane to a sudden stop. There is a certain fatalism about the immediate feeling of relief that overtakes the pilot at this point: his plane has lost so much speed that it could not fly if the arresting cable were somehow to come apart. Not infrequently, the tailhook catches a wire before the wheels have touched, literally snatching his plane out of the air and smashing it to the deck with violence barely short of destruction. Even this conclusion to his flight is welcome, considering that the alternative might be skittering over the forward edge of the flight deck. Once on deck, the pilot must lose no time following the signaled instructions of a "director" in a yellow jersey to get his plane off the landing runway. Someone else is already on the ball, only seconds behind him, and "pri-fly" (primary flight control) may have no more than five seconds to decide between giving a "foul deck" signal or letting the following plane land. The moment the director indicates that his tailhook is clear, the pilot raises it, folds his wings, gently guns his jets and steers where he is directed. Not until his "bird" is safely tied down with chains can the pilot's personal letdown begin. His pulse has slowed by the time he is in the intelligence center for debriefing, and he is plumbing the depths of exhaustion. But debrief he must; operations immediately following may depend on what he has seen and done.

Handling the flight deck is a full-time job, second in importance only to conning the ship herself. Accordingly, the carrier's island is built with what at first glance looks like a second bridge, but it faces to port, over the flight deck, instead of ahead. Pri-fly, as the place is called, is the station where the "air boss" and his assistant, the "mini boss," both naval aviators assigned to the ship's company instead of to an aircraft squadron, perform their jobs as air operations and flight deck controllers. Sometimes, when planes are landing at the rate of two per minute, decisions must be instantaneous, dictatorial—and right every time. During busy periods there may be as many as 300 flights per day, and the tensions, coming one on top of another in rapid-fire sequence, wear relentlessly on the two bosses. At such times they can hardly leave their posts for any reason, nor would either wish to, since responsibility for the safety and proper operation of the entire flight deck rests with them. They are connected with all parts of the deck by telephone, radio and loudspeaker, and must issue instructions to hundreds of people in many separate gangs at the same time. In no other position do the personality and drive of one individual, the air boss, directly affect so many so quickly.

Life aboard a carrier is farther removed from the sea than in any other type of ship. Many crewmen live and work entirely below decks within the community of their divisions. In a ship whose complement may number nearly 6,500 souls, there are many such divisions, some as remote as foreign countries. Men may go for days without seeing or thinking of the divisions in other parts of the ship or, indeed, of the sea itself. A carrier is so big that even at flank speed, i.e., with throttles wide open, the only sensation of movement is the strong wind that sweeps over exposed persons on deck. Her wake, a tremendous white ribbon of tumultuous water eight traffic lanes wide and stretching for miles astern, might as well be from another ship. If full rudder is applied at speed, she will heel away from the turn as any surface ship will, but since her flight deck is over 250 feet wide, men topside will sense no more than a change in the customary location of the horizon. Below, where there are no portholes, people will usually feel only a temporary deflection in the direction of gravity. Similarly, weather is hardly ever noticed by those below; a strong gale may cause a slight roll, perhaps gentle pitching if the great driving hull is in the right resonance with the seas. Some crew members feel impelled on such occasions to go topside to observe; others do not concern themselves about the weather at all, so long as the unaccustomed motion does not make them seasick.

Not everyone needs to experience the sea in the same way. On board a big carrier there are many ways to do so. Some men have it within them to seek adventure and the intensely physical jobs; others look for order and organization, the intellectual challenge of conquering some arcane "glitch" in an electronic circuit, or the satisfaction of preparing good food. A carrier has repair facilities, computer workshops, factories, restaurants, fast-food shops and soda fountains ("geedunk stands"), but no bars or nightclubs. She has ship's police, a jail, courts of law, a chapel, a chaplain and regular church services. There are doctors, dentists, a fully equipped hospital, trained emergency crews and facilities for instant air evacuation of seriously ill or injured persons. Other

Facing: The F/A-18 Hornet is a controversial plane that advocates expect will be proved in operation. The Hornet, with its versatility as both a fighter and a bomber, will replace two older planes in the inventory.

42–43: *An aircraft maintenance man, in green shirt, white helmet and white checkered vest, makes a final check just before this A-7 Corsair is catapulted. Visible are two extra fuel tanks, secured to wing pylons.*

44–45: *Looking up the heat wave as an F-4 Phantom is hurled aloft. The scorching blast of its jets at full power drives particles of loose grit from the nonskid deck surface hundreds of feet aft with painful force.*

Although strict rules and marked boundaries regulate the movements of all who are permitted on the deck, and of the aircraft they service, more than one unwary sailor has been struck by flying debris or blown off the flight deck by an unexpected jet blast. These risks are unavoidable, for trained men must be immediately at hand to help disengage tailhooks and instruct taxiing planes where to go, where to park, where to get fuel. Otherwise there is no way a 750-foot runway can take aboard a twelve-plane flight of 30-ton, twin-jet aircraft at half-minute landing intervals. Similarly, only with someone to guide the launch bar into "the box" for engagement with the catapult, another to set the "holdback" bar with the correct breakable link (to prevent a plane from moving prematurely down the catapult track), others to elevate the jet blast deflectors behind the plane, and still others to check all external surfaces and fittings—to name only a few of the necessary operations—can planes be blasted into the sky every 30 seconds.

Some forty men are usually involved in preparing a "cat" shot. In the roaring noise of a fast-working deck, the familiar thumbs-up signal sprouts like mushrooms as each man completes his checkoff duties. When all hands are clear and the catapult officer is ready, he holds up two fingers and rotates his hand (at night a green flashlight wand) to tell the pilot to rev up his engines. In response, the plane thunders its full power against the jet blast deflector, a hydraulically raised, hinged section of the armored flight deck. With his jets roaring, the pilot operates his controls one last time. When satisfied, he sets them in the prescribed catapult position and salutes the catapult officer, who has been watching him and who salutes back. At night, the plane's wingtip and tail lights, turned on at this moment, take the place of the salute and are acknowledged by a wave of the wand. Then the cat officer makes a final check for anyone who is out of place or has suddenly seen something amiss; he looks specifically to see if his operator at the catapult control panel on the edge of the flight deck is signifying readiness. All being well, he bends down and touches the deck very deliber-

ately with his hand, knuckle or green wand. From this moment on, no one but he or the cat operator can delay the march of events, and that only by halting the prescribed choreography. Then, still in a semi-crouch, the catapult officer thrusts his torso, arm, hand and wand in a forward point. This is the signal the cat operator is waiting for. Solemnly, he looks forward and aft, makes a final check of his gauges, and slams the palm-size launch button with the flat of his right hand.

Below the flight deck, a massive valve crashes open with an explosive sound, shaking the entire fore part of the ship. A great volume of steam, stored in a reservoir at hundreds of pounds of pressure, delivers a sledgehammer blow to the catapult piston. The holdback link resists a fraction of a second, then snaps. Blowing steam the length of its track, the catapult shuttle literally flings the plane into the air. The pilot, already settled back firmly, head against the headrest, feels his seat leap against him. The elastic in his helmet presses hard against his head, the blood drains from his arms and legs, his hand on the control stick tingles from lack of circulation. The plane is designed to fly itself for the first few seconds after takeoff. Were he to hazard a quick backward glance, he would see the carrier deck small and far behind. He is already alone in the sky.

A normal day's flight schedule begins invariably at or a little before dawn. The first aircraft to take off from a carrier's crowded flight deck is the plane guard helicopter. This helo, periodically relieved, keeps station a couple of miles distant on the carrier's starboard beam at low altitude, where it is prepared with trained personnel to rescue any pilot unfortunate enough to end up in the water during flight operations. Second to take off are several E-2 Hawkeyes, long-range high-endurance radar platforms that have prescribed stations around the carrier and, via data link with her CIC, provide her with complete radar coverage within a radius of about 300 miles. Nothing can move within that umbrella without being tracked and, if necessary, acted on by the CIC watch team.

The seventh of December 1941 witnessed a revolution in the balance of forces that comprised the U.S. Navy. When the Pearl Harbor attack wiped out the Pacific Fleet's traditional battle line, America was compelled to concentrate on developing naval air power to match that of the instrument of destruction, Japan. Thus did the U.S. aircraft carrier come into her own. If her coronation was a hard one to accept, it was also a blessing: the air power that she was able to project to distant areas freed the navy from having to rely for its major offensive prowess on guns shackled to surface ships. The main battery of this new capital ship, in contrast to that of the old battleship, was and is her aircraft, or as naval aviators say, her air wing. With it, naval capabilities expanded into dimensions undreamed of by anyone except inveterate aircraft enthusiasts, of whom, by good fortune, the U.S. Navy possessed a substantial number.

The carrier's "mobile battery" catapulted the U.S. Navy into a bold new era of unprecedented sea power, but it did not do so without bringing in its wake certain constraints. The old battleship may have been in the service of her huge turreted rifles, but she was never a slave to them; the carrier, on the other hand, must be entirely devoted to the operation of her air wing. Gone are the quiet maintenance periods of yore. An aircraft carrier under way is flying planes nearly all the time, sometimes twenty-four hours a day. Her catapults, arresting gear engines, deck-edge elevators, flight deck tractors, jet blast deflectors, fuel-pumping stations, ammunition-loading and -unloading equipment and fire-fighting gear are in full operation whenever her planes are in the air. Everything aboard is running continuously. The carrier is a huge, multi-faceted, floating machine shop and, except in special areas, she looks like one, smells like one and feels like one. It is estimated that more than half the space in every aircraft carrier is devoted to machinery necessary for the direct support of flying. This includes everything above the waterline and much of that below. Carriers are so single-mindedly dedicated to their purpose that those who man them are unique among navy crews.

Their pride lies in their ability to handle aircraft swiftly and safely, and although this requires a lot from them, the effort is nothing measured against the lives of the pilots they hold in their hands. There can be no half measures so far as handling planes is concerned; the carrier is always in a state of urgency.

Central to the business of flying aircraft from a carrier is the way they are launched. Some light planes used for mail, high-priority cargo and passengers still roll down the flight deck and fly off the end of it. Helicopters simply lift off from clear spots on the deck edge. Loaded combat jets, however, must be catapulted in order to attain flying speed. With the extraordinary weight and bulk of ordnance they carry under their wings, there is no other way to reach the 150 or more knots of speed they need to become airborne. At the beginning of the flight cycle, under the forward end of the flight deck, the men setting the pressures for each individual launch in the heat of a catapult steam-control room know that too little pressure will drop a plane into the water dead ahead of their speeding ship and too much could tear off its nosewheel or a piece of its wing before hurling it over the ship's bow. Failure either way can lead to disaster. Nothing is quite so fearsome as the sight of a 90,000-ton carrier, 250 feet wide overall, 130 feet wide at the waterline, coming directly toward one at 30 knots. A solid steel wall pushing a mass of water in front of her, she is an implacable juggernaught.

Topside, the flight deck crewmen, all volunteers, race about on the deck in tropic heat or arctic blizzard, dodging the burning hurricanes of jet blasts from planes maneuvering only feet from them. They wear goggles, articulated helmets called cranial protectors, color-coded jerseys to identify their functions, and ear protectors. Supervisors wear radio headsets. The noise on deck, high pitched, loud and never ending, eliminates the possibility of most voice communication; body and hand signals, which can be understood at a distance, are used to direct the action. The unconscious choreography of this silent language would do credit to Radio City Music Hall.

Preceding: The USS Eisenhower, Virginia, South Carolina *and* California *in close formation. The planes on the* Eisenhower's *deck are carefully "spotted" for the morning's flight operations. One is on a waist catapult ready for launching.*

Facing: The USS Saratoga *in the Caribbean Sea. Planes identifiable on her flight deck near the stern are three E-2C Hawkeyes, equipped with early-warning radar, and RA-5C Vigilantes and F-4 Phantoms clustered before and abaft her island.*

Air Power:

Sea Power's
Upper Reaches

tinually arise. One MAU is thus always deployed with the Sixth Fleet in the Mediterranean, ready to begin landing by helicopter at a crisis point within twenty-four hours. The next larger MAGTF (marine air-ground task force, pronounced *magtaf*) is built around a MAB (marine amphibious brigade). The largest possible MAGTF is built around a MAF (marine amphibious force).

There are three MAFs, with about 50,000 men apiece, one headquartered on each coast of the United States and one in Okinawa, Japan, with a portion rear based in Hawaii. The MAFs are ready to be sent anywhere the need for them may arise. But though these forces can cope with troubles in small countries, 50,000 good men, or even all three of the amphibious forces combined, may not be enough to handle some of today's bigger problems. For these, some other sort of force, bringing together components from all of our armed services, may be needed. This was the thinking behind the concept of the Rapid Deployment Force, or as it was later christened, the Rapid Deployment Joint Task Force (RDJTF). When the RDJTF was being formed early in the Carter administration, the marine corps lost no time volunteering its three amphibious forces, pointing out that they were already in place and organized for exactly such a purpose. The other services reacted with nearly equal speed, for each had its own special forces able to accomplish at least a part of the task force objectives. As it is presently constituted, the RDJTF includes airborne, air assault, mechanized infantry, ranger and special forces from the army; any one or all of the three MAFs held in permanent readiness, plus the necessary naval amphibious ships or battle groups to take them where needed; and tactical fighter, reconnaissance and airlift elements from the air force. No new combat units were created; functional units from all the services were simply identified, and a unified command organization was set up.

Not all of the navy's sea-to-land expertise is concentrated in its marine corps. The navy has other amphibious components as well, consisting of the crews

Finding these marines can be a little difficult. On occasion they will live for weeks unaided behind enemy lines. Crack shots, they are sometimes designated for general sniper duty but may well have specific enemy officers or personalities as objectives.

and ships that will transport the marine landing forces to the beaches. The unusual types of ships built during World War II, the most well known being the famous tank landing ship with the "swinging barn door" bow, are still with us today, but mostly in a far more effective guise. The new LST has a sharp bow, makes twice as much speed as the old one, and swings her bow ramp ashore through a pair of great derricks. The LHA, the amphibious assault ship about the size and configuration of a World War II aircraft carrier, has a flight deck to handle helicopters and V/STOL aircraft and a well in her stern for launching landing craft. She can send out beach assault and vertical envelopment forces at the same time. There are also command ships, transports, cargo ships, dock-landing ships and a variety of other special-purpose vessels. The navy's contribution, as might be expected, relates to ship handling, positioning and the transportation of forces by sea. To this, as needed, it adds shore bombardment, air cover and ASW protection. Essentially this is no different from what the navy's surface forces have always done. But when these capabilities are married to the marine air-ground assault capability and assisted by total sea control and surveillance over all possible enemy defensive measures, the combined product can be extremely sophisticated.

In recent years much imaginative effort has been devoted to development—not to say invention—of a truly amphibious vehicle, one as at home on the ground as in the water. To date some success has been achieved with amphibious tanks or personnel carriers, but a much larger craft is needed, one able to move at relatively high speed and transport a large cargo of men or equipment an appreciable distance inland before stopping to off-load. Such craft should be functional during darkness and unfavorable weather and be able to return to the sea for succeeding loads. At the present time tests are being made with the air-cushion vehicle, a form of surface effect ship (SES) that rides on the air contained inside large rubber skirts all around its periphery. This high-technology craft does indeed combine speed with the ability to move directly from water onto land, where it disgorges its cargo over bow and stern ramps lowered for the purpose. The examples built so far require much power, expend a lot of fuel for a small payload, make considerable noise and can negotiate only smooth shelving beaches. Obstacles, man-made or natural, will defeat them. Even so, they possess an unprecedented degree of versatility in amphibious operations.

Navy special forces, the UDTs (underwater demolition teams) and the even more highly trained SEAL (sea-air-land) teams—small, elite, hardened groups of men—also have unique sea-to-land capabilities. The men of both outfits undergo the same basic training for in-water missions, but the SEAL teams receive an additional postgraduate course in unconventional warfare. Both UDT and SEAL teams may be released from close-lying submarines and brought into a contested zone, totally submerged, by electric towing devices of the type popularized for scuba divers. The primary function of UDTs is to investigate, locate and, if feasible, destroy natural or man-made underwater obstacles in a planned amphibious assault zone. UDT men may also function as underwater saboteurs, planting explosives on the bottoms of anchored or moored ships or demolishing maritime structures such as dry docks or defensive installations. SEAL teams are not confined to water; they are prepared for land forays as well. On land they may act as saboteurs, snipers or special agents for any of a number of highly classified missions. They may be dropped from clandestine low-flying planes and later snatched out of a jungle by an aircraft that does not land.

Unconventional warfare has been around for millennia. Nearly 2,500 years ago two Greeks, a father and his daughter according to the story, swimming underwater and breathing through reeds, were reputed to have cut the anchor cables of some Persian galleys at night, resulting in their loss to Xerxes just before the decisive Battle of Salamis. Similar missions were carried out in many areas during World War II and are now part of standard, though unorthodox, procedure. Today men can come up out

of the sea trained and equipped with the fearsome weapons of modern technology, ready to take the initiative of surprise and wreak heavy damage on their nation's enemies. They must be thoroughly prepared, to the highest level of scientific attainment in the special fields pertaining to their missions. They must be superb athletes, able to take any kind of privation for hours and days on end while retaining their mental sharpness and physical abilities. Above all, they must be exceptionally motivated, for the demands placed on them by the risk of discovery or, worse, by discovery itself, can be more unconventional, and more strenuous, than any they themselves might be prepared to inflict on an enemy.

It has been well said that the sea is deceptive. Beneath its frequently calm surface seethe the violence and death of the food cycle. The appearance of the land can also belie reality. Beyond a placid sea glimmering benevolently in the sun may lie a shore lush with verdant growth and health. Yet this land may well be torn up inside with the hatred that only a political or religious contest, or a combination of the two, can cause. To stave off the anarchy that besets the terror-stricken population of such an area is one of the ultimate objectives of the U.S. Navy. Its purpose is to project America's purpose: to maintain peace on the seas and thereby on the land. Its goal is achieved with ships, aircraft, machines and, most importantly, highly proficient, trained personnel, including sailors, marines and technicians. None of these components could perform without the assistance of the others. Long ago the marines dismissed the notion of separating from the navy. Had this taken place, the navy would have had to set up another corps to carry out the amphibious functions that are part of its mandate. Without the variety of its special capabilities, each developed to fill an operational need, the navy could not do the task the country has given it. Together, the ships and their crews, the squadrons of aircraft, the marines and the other special warfare groups form an indissoluble part of the U.S. Navy. Together they are the keepers of the sea, serving the cause of the free world through the storm and strife of the modern age.

Facing: Marines are amphibious troops, equally at home on land or at sea, and their ships can put them ashore by air or by boat. They remain armed while on board.

226–27: *These marines are counting cadence as they approach their navy transport. The group spirit of a trained body of men, confident in their strength as a coordinated unit, has to be experienced to be understood.*

Above: A UDT coming ashore for beach reconnaissance at night in a deserted and unwatched area. There is no easy way to hide the boat, so it is left exposed for rapid withdrawal. The men must be off before first light, taking with them all the evidence of their incursion.

Facing, top: Determining water depth, beach type and enemy alertness and locating any obstructions are among the objectives of the UDT. The frigate bringing the men has closed the beach, and the team paddles off madly through a low surf.

Facing, bottom: Sunset offshore. The USS Belleau Wood will dash in at high speed to the landing debarkation zone and there disgorge her 1,900 marines in landing craft through a well in her stern and by helicopters off her flight deck. Air cover and electronic countermeasures are ingredients essential to her success.

230–31: *It has to move like clockwork. Proper timing will mean the difference between success or failure, few or many casualties. These two sections of amphibious tractors make the initial landing. More assault troops follow in a second wave, all released from ships that speed in from over the horizon.*

Above: Marines in the first assault wave speed up to 30 mph along the strand as they head for the beachhead position selected. Second and third waves will follow in unarmored carriers, and some marines will wade ashore. All hurry to get the beachhead established. Once this is done, they will head swiftly inland.

Above, facing: Range practice with the M60 machine gun, the basic marine infantry automatic weapon. The assistant gunner is loading a new belt. Marine riflemen are the backbone of the marine corps. Their training never ceases.

Left: Air-cushion vehicles (ACVs) show great promise of speeding up amphibious landings. The high-technology JEFF–B, an experimental craft, can move rapidly from water directly onto a shelving beach. ACVs use a lot of power and fuel for a 75-ton cargo, but they possess remarkable versatility.

Facing: The Harrier, a marine corps jet, is the first operational V/STOL aircraft in the U.S. armed forces. High fuel expenditure when taking off or landing vertically curtails its action radius, but it is well suited for close-in support of amphibious landings.

Above: Landing vertically allows the Harrier to drop onto a small clearing or between other aircraft on a crowded deck. This jet is the ideal combat aircraft for small carriers or convoyed ships fitted with small landing areas. The British, who used this plane extensively in the Falklands, swear by its combat capabilities.

Left: The LHA, resembling a medium-sized carrier, is the favored assault ship for vertical envelopment because of its large complement of transport helos and troops. Smaller single-rotor helos support the envelopment by serving as gunships and command and control units.

Above: Vertical envelopment refers to troops landing behind an objective via helicopter. Each CH-46 Sea Knight carries about fifteen combat-equipped men. After securing control of their landing zone areas, the airborne marines link up to coordinate with the beach assault.

238–39: *Loaded with combat-ready marines, one wave of airborne assault forces heads for the enemy coast. It may follow a circuitous route to avoid detection. Others will come at carefully planned intervals to secure more objectives or augment the preceding wave.*

Right: The most vulnerable time in a vertical envelopment is the moment of landing itself, when the assault troops are totally exposed. Marines race off their helos as soon as the rear ramps are lowered and dash for cover to set up defense around the landing zone for the next chopper's arrival. Urgency is the order of the day.

Below: Flying low, the next wave appears. Not a marine is in sight, but defenses are established on the ground, close in, while distant gunships guard the fragile assault helos from the air.

Bottom, right: A quick council of war on the terrain. The man with a white hatband is an umpire who will judge disputes and participate in evaluating the effectiveness of the exercise.

242–43: *The marines believe in moving quickly. The fire team is trained in frontal assault techniques (the fire team "rush"), which should in the long run mean fewer casualties and a swifter, more effective outcome. A twelve-man squad makes three fire teams, rushing alternately.*

Below: The just-unloaded M60 tank has stopped at an assembly point. Behind it is an amphibious tractor, facing in the opposite direction.

Facing: The face is that of a youth, but the look is ages old. More important than the expression, however, is the challenge mastered.

246–47: *The SEAL teams are the elite of navy special forces, the most highly trained, the most disciplined. Formed to cope with terrorism and guerrilla warfare, they can function successfully and ruthlessly under the most hazardous conditions.*

Right: Marching all day in mud and rain is no fun, but privations are borne with traditional marine stoicism by both officers and men. In front of this column is an officer whose most recent order was simply "Follow me, men!"

SEAL teams arrive by boat, by helicopter or by parachute. If they come by air, they can be dropped onto land or into water. Infiltration is always at night, recovery generally completed by daybreak. Teams are picked up from close-in waters by speedboat, by submarine farther out, by helo from the water or land, even by a low-flying fixed-wing airplane that snatches a balloon- or rocket-hoisted pickup line and literally jerks the men into the air.

Right: The training of UDTs is identical to that of SEAL teams, except that there is less emphasis on unconventional or paramilitary operations. Beach exploration prior to an amphibious assault, the removal of obstacles, sensor detection and implantation, and hydrographic reconnaissance are among UDT functions.

Below: The speedboat pickup or "snare," with a rubber boat lashed alongside. Swimmers, in line about 50 yards apart, signal by raising their hands. The recovery boat roars by them. Each, in turn, slides his arm through the snare held out for him and is swung into the rubber boat.

Right: With the first swimmer in the boat scrambling clear, the snare man quickly prepares for the next one, waiting ahead. In a single pass a half-dozen or more men can be retrieved.

252–53: *Various sorts of boats may be used for UDT and SEAL team missions, but their universal requirements are high speed, very shallow draft and quiet engines. The two ships in the right background, based at Little Creek, Virginia, are LSTs. The arrangement for landing their bow ramps shows clearly.*

254–55: *The handsome Charles F. Adams, 4,600 tons, launched in the fall of 1959, has given her name to her class of twenty-three guided-missile destroyers. It is dawn, the day's exercises are about to begin, and the profession of the sea continues.*

Notes on Photography

All the photographs in this book were taken with
35mm Leica equipment. The Leica single-lens reflex
system, with SL2, R3 and R4 bodies as appropriate,
was used. Lenses ranged from 19mm to 400mm.
Missile firings, aircraft activity, aerials and other fast-
moving events required a motor drive with the ex-
posure often set on automatic mode. Most interiors
called for the Leica M system, the lenses anywhere
from 21mm to 50mm. Scenes were photographed
with natural light and no filters, though occasionally
some artificial light was added to interiors; care was
taken not to disturb the mood of the normal light
quality. Kodachrome 25 was the primary exterior
film; the higher-speed Ektachromes were employed
for some low-light exteriors and almost all interior
photographs. A tripod and cable release were used
whenever possible. Kodak Laboratories did all the
film processing.

Keepers of the Sea

Photography by Fred J. Maroon

Designed by Charles O. Hyman

Composed at
Modern Typographers, Inc.
Dunedin, Florida

Printed by
Stephenson, Inc.
Alexandria, Virginia

Cloth and leather editions bound by
Nicholstone Book Bindery, Inc.
Nashville, Tennessee